RAPTURE OF LIFE, LOVE & NATURE

An Anthology of Reality Poems

KENNETH R DAMALLY
2021

Acknowledgement

I am indebted to Dr. Susan Lysett-Davis (Dr. Sue)
Whom I consulted with the concept of writing this Anthology.
She was the very first person with whom I had a CONSULTATION
And she became the source of my MOTIVATION
To get out of my PROCRASTINATION
And get this literary COMPILATION
Into PUBLICATION
For ENTERTAINMENT and EDIFICATION.

There are others too numerous to mention
(Including journalists and authors)
That were the source of inspiration to write about
Human behavior, Relationships, Philosophical viewpoints, and Mother Nature.
My sincere thanks to all who contributed directly or indirectly to this publication.

It is said o*nly Irish coffee provides all four essential food groups in a single glass:*
Alcohol, Caffeine, Fat and Sugar:
But this Anthology of Reality Poems provide luminosity for living:
Lyrics, Love, Laughter and Lessons

Dedicated to my mother Etheline Shackleford (1920-2019),
Late Wife Yasmin Damally (1950-2019)
children, grand-children, and great-grand-children.

A creative mind is like a parachute; it only works when it is open. It is not a vessel to be filled, but is a fire to be constantly stoked; and to provide the framework for common-sense logic, analytical and problem-solving prowess. It enables me to realize the power of observing things in an entirely different way.

From that perspective I was able to read a story and if I find humor or inspiration in it, I could immediately create a poem or story-line and produce it into a poem or prose.

Extraordinary and unique experiences give life to everlasting memories.

Hobbies are writing and photography.

Cover Design, Layout, and Photography
- Ken Damally

This book or any part thereof may not be reproduced or distributed in any form without the expressed permission of the author or publisher.

DISCLAIMER

The materials presented in this book were all conceived and compiled by the author – except where duly acknowledged. They are for general entertainment and knowledge only. Any similarities to other published articles, are purely coincidental, and the author shall have no liability or responsibility to any entity or person who allege any likeness to their ideas or photos herein. Where every effort was made to ensure accuracy, there is no implied guarantee.

Email: **rodama3@bellsouth.net**
Fort Lauderdale, Florida

Introduction

"RAPTURE OF LIFE, LOVE, & NATURE" is a fresh realistic and exhilarating outlook at humanity from real-life perspectives, sacred and secular, humor, nature, and some themes about love, romance, and even their dissolution - to tantalize your varied fantasies.

This classic anthology of poems is a creative attempt to relate personal experiences, anecdotes, and philosophical viewpoints with an objective to enhance the reader's experience. Some items were actual events gleaned from news media relating to discord, infractions, barbarity, hilarious news and views, and of the author's ruminations. The stimulatory topics were collected and compiled from real-life experiences, poignant issues that impact the everyday lives of people, observations of, places, and the natural beauty and mystique of the fauna, flora, and other wonderful things that compliment us on this beautiful planet earth.

The short stories, and philosophical quotes are presented in a creative contemporaneous style to highlight the contempt, humor, or the ideals of humanity - and for edification.

These selected poems and prose which speak for themselves, cover a diverse range of human life, while portraying the romantic side of the author, his analytical prowess, passion for natural beauty, luxuriating in the paradisiacal settings of his lush tropical island of Jamaica, West Indies, Florida, and New York City.

In *"RAPTURE OF LIFE, LOVE & NATURE",* you will find a true down-to-earth presentation that hopefully everyone will thoroughly enjoy.

Come gallivant with him on an experiential, picturesque, and poetic journey of facts of life, fun, love, romance, and observations, and it most certainly will make you want to:

EXPLORE, LIVE, LOVE, LAUGH, & LEARN

About the Author

Born in Port Antonio, Portland, Jamaica and attended Nonsuch Primary School.
Attended Port Antonio Technical Institute, a vocational training school for Wood and Metal Work Technology. Graduated 1962.
Enlisted in the Jamaica Defence Force for six years (1963-69), Attained the rank of Lance Corporal.
Attended Kingston Technical High School in 1975, for engineering and accounting studies.
The family migrated to New York City in January of 1980.
Worked with Mount Sinai Medical Center as a Security Officer November 1980 to December 1985.
Graduated from Borough of Manhattan Community College in 1983 with an AAS degree in accounting.
Became a licensed Real Estate associate in Florida with Century 21, Inc. in 1989.
Graduated from Middlesex County College with a Certificate in Technical Writing.
Hobbies are writing and photography.

Hope you will enjoy this poetic journey of fun facts of life, love, and nature from life experience and observations in this **Second Edition.**

Table of Contents

Adulation	10
Personal Quest for Success	11
Autumn Leaves	12
Splendor on Boston Beach, Jamaica	13
Beauty of a Woman	14
A Gem in the Sun	15
The Jamaican Man	16
Break of Day	17
Christmas Time	18
Civility Matters	19
Cranial Citadel	20
Definition of Self	21
Desirable	22
Embrace Love	23
Adam's Malediction	24
Discover Me	25
Canine Coaction	26
Encompassing Beauty	27
Flora	28
Hyacinth	29
Family Values	30
Happy to be Me	31
I Wish You Enough	32
Journey of Life	33
Alluring Beauty	34
Battle for Attention	35
Leggs	36
Land of Love- Jamaica	37
Nucleus of Growth	38
The Incredible Ants	39
Love Supreme	40
Lady Love	41

Aim High	42
Mad Dogs	43
Meditation	44
Mirror of the Soul	45
Mind Your Manners	46
Moon Beams	47
Surreal Dream Lover	48
Night Walk	49
Nuptial Ablation	50
Ode to the Bed	51
Once in a Lifetime	52
Ode to a Dear Mother	53
The Farmer Ants	54
Passport to Freedom	55
Evangelical Malfeasance	56
Power of Words	57
Realization – Who Am I?	58
Shelter of Love	59
Rain on Me	60
Speak to me of Love	61
Supplication	62
Sweet Surrender	63
The Diaper Man	64
Teatime	65
The Canine and the Cock	66
Remodeling a Transgender	67
The Crow and the Pitcher	68
The Manhattan Crowd	69
The Recluse	71
The Rattler	72
The Spanish Needle	73
The Soldier Boy	74
The Toiler's Agony	75
Positive Attitudes	76
Love Quest	77
Together in Love	78
Tropical Treasure	79
Twilight Time	80

What is Mankind?	81
Wake Up People	82
When will we Learn	83
Ode to a Dad	84
A Good Mother	85
Winter Winds	86
Yearning	87
Young People Creed	88
Devotion	89
Meaning of Life	90
Dancing in Lovers Cove	91
The Unforgettable Woman	92
The Back Nine-Dash of Life	93
Congratulations – Graduation	94
Affirmation & Spice of Life	95
Spice of Life	96
Girl From Ipanema (Reprise)	97
Soul Mate	98
Protect Our Children	99
The Young Child	100
Hair	101
Soul Devotion	102
The Life of Grass	103
Ras Tafari	104
Eventide Aura	105
Liberation of Life	106
Falling in Love	107
Our Journey of Life	108
Wasted Lives	109
The Beauty of a Good Wife	110
Qualities of a Beautiful Woman	111
The Power of a Woman	112
Monkey See – Monkey Sue	113
Island of Love – Jamaica	114
Meaning of Life	115
Midnight Kiss	116
Daybreak	117
Beauties on the Beach	118
Don't Be Crude!	119

Corridor of Death	120
The Good Life	121
I Am a Born Jamaican	122
The Five T's	123
The Golden Rules for Living	124
Life & Work Management	125
Finding a Good Man	126
Ladies Decorum	128
Reference Guide to Friends Personality	131
Instruction for Life	134
Philosophy of Life	138
Bungling Bureaucracy	161
ABC of Friendship	164
A Brilliant Anecdote	165
Life's Journey	167
Prayer for Everyone	168

Adulation ©

I like your comely eyes,
They seem so soft and kind.
I like your lovely cheeks,
Your dimples blow my mind.

I like your seductive lips,
A kiss perhaps would tell.
I like your shapely hips,
I admire each curve and swell.

I like your legs and thighs
You walk with such sexy pride.
I like your all to eternity
Such charms with me abide.

I like the exquisite apparel you wear
Your modesty and all that I see
The attractive way you style your hair
Your captive I could easily be.

With such allure and angelic face
I don't want to seem overbearing
A perfect woman of elegance and grace
You're lovely - I'll say it again, and again.

Personal Quest for Success ©

I can be all I want to be,
That is completely up to me.
I can elevate myself up to the sky,
Think positively, and maybe I can fly.
I am ready and open to every opportunity.

I can succeed at whatever I attempt,
Graduate myself to the fullest extent
Won't take anyone or anything for granted.
I'll practice the good values implanted
By my loving ancestors now departed.

I have wisdom to know right from wrong
I make it a point to keep smiling and trusting
To develop a sense of trust and confidence
To crave knowledge and common sense
Knowing I can accomplish my purpose.

I strive to never, ever settle for less,
To desire moral values over material excess.
Grant me O God, control over my faculties and emotions
To execute my plans with a sense of purpose
As I pray for strength to always pursue success.

<u>Autumn Leaves</u> ©

When the autumn leaves leave
And, the cool northern winds arrive,
We know autumn will soon be over;
And most trees slowly shed their attire
Waiting to enjoy a soft snowy shower.

The wintery winds begins to gust
Baring the deciduous trees to the element
Disclosing every avian and cocoon resident.
But shortly they'll again be shrouded
With the deposits of winter's blend.

Winter weather is here, we must make haste!
Hurry! It's prudent for us to emulate
The ants, animals, and everything else.
They gather their chow for sustenance;
As they prepare for the long winter repose.

Splendor on Boston Beach, Jamaica ©

Broiling tropical sun and soft white sand,
The white cresting waves shoreward bound,
Dousing bathers with its saline concoction.
Cooled and dried by the northeasterly wind
It makes an exciting day for the sea, surf, and sun.

The soothing sound of the Caribbean Sea,
The fresh air, and the aquamarine hue,
A reflection of the temperate blue sky,
With the mighty ocean in the distance,
Life on the beach - a totally exhilarating experience.

Multi-colored almond leaves dot each swell
Like rose petals swirling in a luxurious whirlpool.
They dance around the contour of everyone.
People play with each circuitous wave action,
The rotations providing agitation and fun.

Like migrating birds seeking nest and nutrition,
Humans jostle on the beach for the ideal location,
Seeking nature's vitamin D, and a beautiful tan.
They flock to the beaches to congregate
With family & friends to celebrate, or rejuvenate.

Adjoining the picturesque silky white sand mecca,
It is the classic culinary delight center of Jamaica,
The birthplace of jerk chicken, pork, and more,
To satiate your palette with their famous spicy fare,
Then wash it all down with ice-cold coconut water.

Beauty of a Woman ©

The beauty of a woman lies within her,
Not the way she combs her hair.
It's not the pretty clothes she wears,
Or her elegant voluptuous figure.

The beauty of a woman is her zest,
Recognized through her eyes,
The doorway to her heart,
That place where love resides.

The beauty of a woman
Is not her facial mole,
The true beauty in a woman
Is reflected in her soul.

The beauty of a woman is intelligence,
The caring advice she lovingly gives,
Always wearing a pleasing countenance
With each passing year - she only glows.

A Gem in the Sun ©

Jamaica, a jade in the Caribbean Sea,
A land of unique experiences and beauty
With breathtaking landscapes and scenery
A climate ideal for almost any activity
The place to relax, and rejuvenate in harmony.

Wake up at daybreak to hear the roosters crowing,
The birds melodiously chirping or singing
The canines barking, felines meowing
It's wonderful being in my beautiful homeland.
Because I'm a very proud Jamaican.

Our people have made tremendous contributions
In academia, culinary arts, music, and sports.
Skills and talents are here in abundance
Waiting to be discovered and given a chance
To make themselves into proud Jamaicans.

Reggae music playing in every nook and cranny,
Watch the children skanking, even the granny.
A convergence of many cultural diversity
One people with one aim, one shared destiny
That makes Jamaica a place of beauty and prosperity.

The Jamaican Man ©

I'm an affable and proud Jamaican
I was born in Portland
Evolving from a humble beginning
Having gone over three scores and ten
Was never swayed by material things,
Always grateful for family and good friends.

Yes! I experienced setbacks and disappointments
But, like a phoenix I gracefully rose above the fray
Never made them a place of permanent residence
Too blessed to be stressed
Happy to be God's child, alive and healthy.

Do not underrate me because I am gentle,
I engage all my senses with acuity,
My observations are more than you know,
Because I have two eyes to see.
I know and see much more than I say.

I am blessed with two keen ears
To hear human and nature's intonations.
Being the cautious introvert that I am.
I listen more, mesh my brain, before I vocalize
Through one mouth – I engage intellectual discourse

Break of Day ©

As the sun slowly ascends over the craggy mountain,
The bay comes alive with egrets, gulls, and terns.
Awake from their siesta after a tranquil night,
The birds herald the break of dawn,
To frolic and engage in another food fight.

The white-crested waves roll in from the ocean,
The breakers crashing against the cliff,
At times, fading to a faint whisper, then calm;
I paused to ponder the miraculous symmetry of life,
Such soothing aural experience at dawn.

Sunlight glistening off the cresting wavelets
The aerial predators dipping, diving, and soaring
With catches too immense for their gullets.
Frenzied feeding, fighting, and frolicking
Above and around the rocky coastal cliffs.

Perched on the top of exquisite Fern Hill,
I can see the craggy cliffs of Alligator Head
Watching the foamy surfs crashing the shoreline
White-crested waves crashes against the beachhead
And the craggy cliffs above the briny swell.

Christmas Time ©

Christmas time is here again,
The longest celebratory season.
A season of festivities and celebrations
When every child is in full anticipation.
For a plethora of goodies for the stocking.

The cool northern winds come to town,
The hydrangeas and poinsettias efflorescence.
Inspirational carols and music abound
Most everywhere are friendly faces
Some in make-belief altruistic mood.

The shelves crammed with Christmas wares,
The merchants ready and eagerly waiting,
To maximize their lackluster profit margin.
It's the season when common sense accedes to excess
Materialism, lust and greed become obvious.

When all the joyous spending takes hiatus,
Only the merchants and children are cheerful.
Some spouses usually start raucous fuss,
Caused from the other's overindulgence
For the Christian festival of Christmas

Civility Matters ©

Civility is more than polite courtesies,
It enables us to live respectfully in communities
Regardless of our age, it is the glue that binds society.
It can be the difference between life and death – literally.
Acknowledge kindness, gratitude and generosity.

Engage in dialogue by phone or face-to-face visits.
Develop interpersonal skills and relationships
Enrich and nurture social connections
Whether in academia, in the home, or the business
They are an accurate predictor of future success.

Embrace meditative and teachable moments
Encourage common sense, decency, and fairness.
We can promote decorum, ethics and morality.
Let us plant the seeds for future generation.
Our existence and livelihood depend on Civility.

Cranial Citadel ©

Cradled deep inside the cranial cavity,
Embedded the sensory control center of human.
The most complex organ in the body,
This nucleus of intellectual activity,
Manages our grief, pleasure, laughter or pain.

To the brain, we owe all our movements,
It is the regulator of human survival;
Love, emotion, fear, fright or flight
Without it, this poem would be naught
Speech would be just a babble or a grunt.

The brain controls our diverse personality,
All cognitive functions and creative ability.
A dynamic depot of mental acuity
It directs all physical and physiological action.
It is our brain that elevates us human.

The brain is the most complex computer
The generator for the power of logic
Filled with encyclopedic volume of data,
To design and fabricate eclectic environs
And everything pertinent to our existence.

Definition of Self ©

Yes! I may be an introvert, but I'm not shy,
I'm not stuck up, just want to live sociably
I 'm not antisocial, just careful of my cohorts
I'd rather be home with a few close confidants
Than a crowd of so-called friends.
If I open myself up to you, you are special indeed.

I have two eyes – to observe our universe,
And to sit by the window and read;
To broaden my perspective on issues.
I have two ears - to listen and learn,
Analyze my inner self, meditate and understand.
To live a good life, laugh, and love everyone.

I have one mouth – no time for petty gossip,
I will talk for hours about life and fellowship.
I dislike being governed by materiality,
Or by the artificial restraints of humanity.
Respect that I'm reserved, and trustworthy.
Accept me as I am – I am Venus's prodigy!

<u>Desirable</u> ©

Stirred by the fires of my emotion,
My thoughts converge on you.
Consumed by intense desire,
Bewitched and enthralled by your devotion,
I drift into the enticing world of thy being.

Your charm and brilliance captivate me,
Your good looks and personality too.
Engaging discourse and a sense of humor,
Desirable qualities I yearn for in a woman.
To share a life of absolute fervor.

Burying my face between the rising mounds,
Is like the soft summer cloud in the heavens.
As I listen to your soft alluring voice,
You must have been sent from above
To elevate my spirit – yes, I am in love.

<u>Embrace Love</u> ©

Whenever there is a vacuum in your life,
Let love fill that emptiness.
When tribulation leave you sullen,
Let love be your state of being.

When life has drained you, go seek love joyfully,
Love is natural, invigorating and pure,
The vital energy transforms the whole personality
Love is not only enticing, but also a cure.

Whenever you are feeling spiritually helpless,
Reach out and touch someone.
Love encompasses, fulfills, and enriches.
Love will help you overcome.

Love lives, breathes and grows in a state of peace.
Love is the gateway to true happiness.
Young, old or middle-aged, fill up on love
Love creates a path to lasting bliss.

Adam's Malediction ©

What a tribalism and tribulation on the land!
Ever since the creation of mankind,
Constant conflicts among every nation,
Proliferation in weapons of mass destruction
With each succeeding generation.

There are conflicts of sectarianism
Politicians and people against pluralism
Even the people in journalism
Get caught up in the schism
Everyone advancing their own idealism.

People of the world are in rebellion,
Increased inter-factions' castigation
Exhorting their own brand of indoctrination,
And with the advent of electronic media,
All and sundry proffer their vitriolic idea.

Yes, human are imperfect creatures,
Some think they are God's gladiators.
They become more volatile predators,
When given guns and ammunitions,
Resulting in a divergence of tribal tribulation.

They spread destruction and hate
In the name of ill-conceived caliphates,
They care less about the citizens' fate
To legitimize their artificial façades
Decimating people of every other faith.

Discover Me ©

Yes! People say I am Mom's only son,
Who is handsome, shy, and debonair;
The ambitious and exploring one
But I am uniquely me – the analyzer.

I crave the simple life, free from falsity
A life full of fun and risibility
Embracing genuine friends and family
I crave beauty, peace, love and symmetry.

I adore affable children and women
Have a noble penchant for a modest life
I ignore white noise or petty concern
I thrive on positive vibes - free from strife.

I seek an intellectual and spiritual relationship,
Not material extravagance or luxury,
Tend to be too optimistic, and trusting in kinship,
And attract people with questionable affinity.

My energy comes from the sun,
The waves of the ocean are like my emotion.
The wonders of the heavens embrace my mind,
Music of varying genre and tempo is my passion.

I listen to the birds singing their varied cantatas,
Watch the bees engaging every flower
Sniff the delicate fragrance of jasmine and roses
And yearn for the good life - always and forever.

Canine Coaction ©

The midsummer night was usually tranquil
When a bark breaks the serenity of the community.
Pronto; our cute and docile border collie
So humanlike and loyal in his social acuity
Sprinted to the gate for his protective guard duty.

The signal reverberates like a relay message,
Like drum signals used by our early ancestors,
Or as Morse code in telegraphic missives,
Our canine friends use varying frequencies,
Like an assorted mélange of coordinating codex.

Signals vary for attack, fight, flight, or pain.
A bark, or growl for those held in disdain.
Their plaintive signals at the speed of sound,
Fast aggressive barks to signal an intruder.
Barks of welcome, or warning to any visitor,

Canines are adored for their olfactory attributes.
Use body languages to signal their delight,
With a whimper or wiggery tail for greetings.
A snarl, eyeing, or retreat mode to signal disgust,
They make for us excellent human companions.

<u>Encompassing Beauty</u> ©

Most men crave beautiful things to admire
Unending quest to acquire ultimate pleasure.
They wheedle women of exquisite beauty
By catering to their every dream of splendor
Wagering assets to satisfy his salacious fancy.

Comparable to the myriad species of exquisite rose
So are women's seemingly sweet repose.
They can be like jewels waiting for a suitor.
To cherish the goodness within her
And to embrace her mystique and glamour.

Men build castles like the Casa Amore
And lavish his conquest with exquisite luxury
The finest furs and magnificent must-haves
Explore exotic places of endless pleasure
For golden moments in the garden of love.

Photo by Ken Damally

<u>Flora</u> ©

Star of the earth, you radiate classic splendor,
The most wonderful gift from the creator
Intricately cultured for everyone to adore
You are nature's finest universal exhibition.
The most brilliant star at every wedding.

Your omnipresence adorns every occasion,
Dinner dates for two, or even a million,
Be it formal, informal, sacred or secular.
You embellish homes, palaces and in between,
Emblazon books, merchandise and magazine.

The daffodils, lilacs, lilies and anthurium,
Azaleas, buttercups, ferns and roses.
Daisies, begonias, pansies, geraniums,
Making a showy lake or pool of color
In which to have an exhilarating swim.

The birds and bees imbibe your nectar
Your plethora of fragrances often replicated.
You offer cheer and serenity to the afflicted.
Moreover Flora, when the toil of life is over
You accompany the spirit of the dearly departed.

Photo by Ken Damally

Hyacinth ©

There she grows; a creation of true elegance
Delicately crafted by nature's guidance
Exuding the sweetest fragrance
She adorns the earth for everyone
Part of nature's finest attractions.

In the springtime she effloresces,
The centerpiece of any romantic garden.
Her alluring beauty enchants the birds and bees
Courting, flirting, while extracting the juices
From all the flowers that fill our Garden of Eden.

Your cousins are equally precious,
Crocus, daffodils, gladiolus and iris,
A conglomeration of classic beauty
Each contributing their own exquisite hue
Where lovers can stroll in an air of ecstasy.

Family Values ©

Abundant fruits begin with healthy shoots
Nurture and tender the orchard well.
It is not the quantity that really counts
Although we prefer to reap by the bushel
We need an orchard that yield pleasant fruits.

One generation passes, and another is born
A family of character and integrity
Will certainly sustain the extension
Civility can save lives – literally,
Nurture children and encourage education.

Embrace attitudes that are true and just,
Things that are sincere, pure and lovely
Whatever things that are exemplary
Strive for wisdom; it is better than folly.
Accept responsibility and show respect.

Forests grow from good quality off-springs,
Groom the young to grasp opportunities
Nurtured seedlings become magnificent foliage.
Give them the tool to develop their communities
Let's all be guardians for ourselves and families.

Happy To be Me

I am who I am, intricately made.
I may have imperfections tenfold,
But I am a part of God's creation.
I just need patience and cooperation.
I am happy to be me, a Libran.

I am not a bragger or try to impress anyone,
Animosity and fallacy I do not condone.
Help me to understand your perception,
I always crave a good conversation,
Give me your undivided attention.

You can counsel and guide me,
You may help me to improve me,
Nevertheless, you just cannot alter me.
Accept me as I am, I give the best of me.
I am nature's child, as happy as can be.

I am a man, and I am fallible,
I am honest, loving and happy.
Appreciate me and teach me plenty.
I am happy and will always seek peace.
On my sojourn through the universe.

I Wish You Enough ©

I wish you enough sun to keep your attitude bright,
No matter how gray the day may appear you will see the light.
I wish you enough happiness to keep your spirit alive and everlasting.
I wish you enough gain to satisfy your wanting.
Enough ethics to be honest with yourself and the other person.
I wish you enough fortitude to withstand adversity and temptation.
Enough knowledge to know the tremendous benefits of gratitude.
I wish you enough patience to persist until you succeed.
Enough wisdom to differentiate your wants from your needs.
Enough fervor to get people to smile, and enamor new friends.
I wish for you not to worry and have wrinkles, smile and have dimples.
Take enough time to walk in the beautiful garden and smell the flowers.
I wish you enough loss to appreciate all that you possess.
Enough hope to be immune to despair or disease.
I wish you enough courage to be impervious to mediocrity.
I wish you enough foresight to avoid obstacles and debauchery.
I wish you enough rain to appreciate the sun even more.
I wish you enough time to meditate and appreciate nature.
I wish enough health to reach the prize of life at the end of the journey.
I wish you enough hellos to get you through the final good-bye.

<u>Journey of Life</u> ©

The journey of life is not an easy corridor,
From conception through to entombment.
It has a plethora of obstacles to conquer.
Life embodies a maze of intricate orbit,
But faith will definitely help us to prevail,
As we navigate the highway, and the dark trail.

Everyone has an impact on humanity,
Regardless of the prevailing status quo
Continue to forge doors of opportunity,
Blazing trails for those that follow
Seize to chance to provide a lasting legacy,
The door for an opening to grow.

Human live to procreate, but some are asexual,
As one generation passes away, another muster,
Mankind is like a flower destined to fall
But the earth certainly lives on forever.
As we sojourn through the universe
. Live and love responsibly to our utmost,

Alluring Beauty ©

Kind, intelligent, loving, sentient, and receptive,
Your sensuous gait so uniquely expressive.
I like the elegant attire you wear,
The way you style your hair - so attractive.

Your quiet style, poise and personality,
Like a flower yielding its nectar to a bee
You take my breath away - so comely
How easy I could be your captive be.

I love your smile, your face, and your eyes
Exuding loving beauty, you float with grace;
Having such allure, and angelic face;
I want to feel your sweet embrace;

I don't want to appear overbearing,
My feelings for you is hard to explain
It's one of fond affection, and appreciation
When I say it again, and again;
You're lovely is my lasting refrain.

When I close my eyes in rumination
I think of your loveliness and charms,
My spirit is as restless as the ocean
Yearning to engulf you in my arms.
As an affirmation of my admiration.

Battle for Attention ©

The evolution of the digital delivery system
Created dormancy in some people's cranium
Almost everyone is into I-cloud
Sexting, tapping, texting away on their I-Pads
Imitating the birds with their tweets,
Some divulging their intimate secrets,
Lost in a state of nonverbal wilderness.

The modern world of electronic gadgets
Facilitates a wider dissemination of news and views,
Secular, sacred, and salacious missives.
People become ever more selfish and vainer
Exposing every facet of their lives on I-phone.
Seldom able to engage in a good conversation
Without a gadget competing for attention.

Courtesy www.picsearch.org

Leggs ©

Oh, gorgeous stanchions of grace,
The patent of women with poise and beauty.
Enhancing chic, smart attire of elegance,
The focal point of every man's idolatry.

They adorn and support her curvaceous figure,
Artfully appended to her sybaritic thighs.
Enshrining and protecting her esteemed vulva.
Like exquisite gold ornate pillars.

Legs are the ultimate essence of every model
And some very famous performers
With eyes and smiles that sparkle
Complimenting their curvature and accessories.

With them she travels the world over,
And when she is ready, and the fervor is right,
Enable her to embrace and envelop her paramour,
The moment she wishes to excite, or to procreate.

Land of Love – Jamaica ©

When the sun finally sets over the horizon,
And the night spread its wings over the land,
I watched the moon rises over the Blue Mountains,
Shedding its soft silvery light over the lush terrain.
Another hectic day comes to an end.

The Rio Grande shimmering through the plains,
The falls whisper under the magical moon beams,
As the glistening water rushes to meet the briny foam
With fresh mineral water from the mountains
To replenish and neutralize the ocean.

As the diurnal avian bid their plaintive farewell
Out comes the bats, cicadas, fireflies, and owls
Taking their turn to explore, frolic, and feed.
While some bipeds and quadrupeds retire to bed
For a rejuvenating rest, and quiet repose.

Occasionally, the tranquility of the night is broken
By the chatter and laughter of lovers, or a vehicle.
The nightingales singing their parting refrain
Serenading the children who are home from school
Finishing homework, listen folk tales, or read the Bible.

Prayers said, goodnight kisses, sweet dreams wish,
Ablution completed, nighties and pajamas on,
Lovingly they are tucked in their humble cluster.
When morning breaks, it's time again
To rise, shine, duties, and muster.

Nucleus of Growth ©

Forests effloresce when seeds evolve.
Nurtured seedlings form magnificent foliage.
Matured embryos bear parental attributes
Likewise, the genetics of every creature,
Characteristics that survive life's passage.

The gigantic oak began from a tiny acorn
Raindrops feed a creek, to a river, to the ocean.
Grandiose edifices evolved from the tip of a pen.
Nations are built from the blood, sweat and tears,
With the combined efforts of patriotic citizens.

As the sunrise predicts the day at dawn
So is the youth for the next generation.
When youths are trained to take responsibility,
That begins the creation of a viable society.
Their talent and skills bring economic prosperity.

The Incredible Ants ©

Ever observe the ingenuity of social insects,
The most incredulous complex creatures ever?
Their signals travel over their entire empire,
To summon colleagues for a gourmet treasure.

When a scout makes a sumptuous find,
Regardless of the distance from the colony
A signal is sent to everyone in the domain
Then suddenly, an army converge on the prey.

Quickly they surround the hapless invertebrate.
Working in complete unison they haul the worm,
Surmounting any obstacle regardless of gradient
In absolute unity, destined for their cozy dorm.

Pretty soon every ant is out of sight.
The hunt expertly done for the party,
Their feast taken without a fight,
The incredible ants restock their pantry.

Love Supreme ©

I have found you sweetheart, found you,
So kind, intelligent and sentient.
I found a love supreme and true,
Maybe your charms were from heaven sent.

I have found you, yes I have found you,
A modest lady, serene and kind.
Have God-given richness and virtue,
Qualities that are hard to find.

I have found you, dearest, found you,
Found two hands of tender touch.
Soft lips, cheeks, and a petite figure,
Overwhelming qualities, I crave so much.

I have found you, beloved, found you,
You fill me with joy and pride.
You make my whole being - emerge anew,
I want you always to be by my side.

Courtesy www.picsearch.org

Lady Love ©

He ogled her every sensuous stride.
As she sashayed down the street,
Allowing his imagination to run wild,
His salacious desire causes him to lust.

He yearns for a moment to chat with her,
Maybe a drink from her well-spring of love potion,
Or a chance to satisfy his insatiable desire,
And imbibe the sweet nectar from her fountain.

He is not a libertine, or a promiscuous man,
Neither is he an Adonis or a Don Juan,
He just wants a real friend to call his queen.
And his very own exotic, and exquisite cistern

He seeks a mate with poise and sensuality,
A lady who is compatible and brainy
Who exudes charm, modesty and spirituality
A woman that embodies peace, love and virtue.

Aim High ©

Like branches on a tree
We grow in different directions
Yet our roots remain as one.
We are destined to yield fruit in abundance
Nurture our roots with love and understanding.
We must stand up, and take a positive stance.

Let your dream and ambition take flight
Like an eagle soaring high
Aim high and shoot for that target
Take positive steps to avert poverty
Be not afraid of any rapacious cohort
Live ethically and strive for prosperity.

Ambition and hard work is paramount.
Rise above all adversities, and recognize your worth.
Distracters and pessimists will always be present.
Show respect and gratitude to everyone.
Recognize that preparation and opportunity lead to fortune.
Ignore the messiahs of apathy and stagnation.

Mad-Dogs ©

Why do us in our midst
Allow repugnant bipeds to run wild.
They prey on decent and productive citizens,
Death and destruction, they leave behind.

With automatic weapons and bombs exploding,
People losing life and limbs,
Even the lower animals cowering,
As the nations' death toll, continue to climb.

Daily we hear dispatched emergency vehicles,
Some hapless souls fall victims of crime,
Inundating the police, doctors and paramedics,
Hey! The mad-dogs strike again!

No compassion, love, respect or solace,
Are known in their anarchistic core,
When other innocent humans are effaced,
Curtailing everyone's right to endure.

Occasionally they are apprehended and caged,
Fed and made comfortable in style,
While the community is bereaved
Because of the mad-dogs were running wild.

Soon they are scrutinized and bargained for,
Accorded the rights they deny other citizens,
By an influential, intellectual charlatan,
Then let loose again to continue their wanton killing.

Courtesy www.picsearch.org

Meditation ©

Ascending the magnificent Mount Oriole,
The cool mountain air caressing my face
Captivating my body and soul,
A feeling of well-being and peace,
My ultimate sense of providence.

From the heights of my sanctuary,
I marveled at the lush green landscape
Interspersed with the farms and pastures,
The magnificent fields of camellias
I reconciled the symmetry of life and nature.

Here on cloud nine I find spiritual comfort,
Where I can increase my mental capacity,
Experiencing my inner being in absolute clarity,
Relieving stress, and enhancing my spirituality.
Meditation is for physical focus and tranquility.

Courtesy www.picsearch.org

Mirror of the Soul ©

My most precious nucleus of existence,
You are the windows on the world.
Often gleam with such exquisite brilliance.
With the power to penetrate, and seduce,
Able to conceal, and reveal every mood.

An integral organ of every human and minion,
Created in a plethora of colors and shapes,
Can show health, joy, pain, or passion;
Also can enchant, scare, or show contempt.
Or evince feelings of love or conflict.

Eyes can be mysterious, and misconceived.
Not every twinkle or thought can be read.
When an active day is concluded,
They close out the world and its beauty.
And when life is ended, they gently close for eternity

Mind Your Manners ©

Let your actions shine like a beacon,
That radiate your goodness from within.
Refrain from being extraordinarily loud,
And honor seniors to make them proud.
Civility is a requisite to calm a savage world.

Let your smile flash like the lightening,
So that it illuminates the path of everyone.
Intelligence will attract positive people,
Then consensus, favor and success will prevail.
Show assertiveness with respect to all.

Let your voice roll like thunder,
Not with obscenities, deceit, destruction or hate,
Use words of inspiration and love for another.
Embrace peaceful coexistence with consorts,
Never forgetting to smile - it is contagious.

Let your oration reveal your intellect,
Self-respect and demeanor is paramount.
Never fall under the influence of the dust,
Nor create any morose entanglement.
Comradery elevates the human spirit.

Moon beams ©

Softly the shadows around us wane,
The sun descends over the western province.
The nocturnal creatures appear on the scene,
As their diurnal colleagues depart for respite.
What a tranquil setting; for a splendid night.

The moon bathes the earth with its silvery light,
The stars begin to dance in the cloudless sky,
As I embrace my lady passionately.
Listening to the serenade of the nocturnal guests,
As they emerge to feed, frolic and procreate.

Their eclectic renditions - a melodic aura,
From nature's nocturnal orchestra,
Synchronizing the rhythm of life and nature.
They are all entertaining for our aural pleasure.
Concurrent with the sound of the flowing river.

The fireflies hover like blue-green flashing stars
Illuminating everywhere - not lit by the moon.
The owls enquiring about our presence
In their winged world of the garden,
As the breeze tickles and teases our face.

My Surreal Lover ©

It was one chimerical moonlit night,
While promenading in Dover's landing,
Holding my lady in a passionate embrace.
And marveled at the vista of Spanish Town;
When she called my name in an alluring tone.

I was captivated by her decorum
Under the seductive light of the moon
The night blooms cast a magic potion
Creating a perfect romantic setting
When it was curtailed by a female intone.

Suddenly the surreal became real,
The enamoring voice was quite literal,
Awakened by the real lady
Hailing me, under my bedroom window,
In the crisp, cool morning air of Mercury.

My lady love was a real angel of mercy,
Summoning my help for a neighbor in labor.
To be an emergency chauffeur
For the mother to the hospital urgently
Just in time to deliver a baby boy.

Night Walk ©

The moonlit night was fascinating,
With the cool northeasterly wind blowing,
Every diurnal creature cease working
Retreating under the light of the seductive moon,
Not mindful of any loving intruders.

Come, let us walk into the garden
Where the gardenia and jasmine are in bloom.
We can observe the celestial wonders,
Take time to smell the fragrant flowers,
And adulate the precious gifts from the creator.

Let's stroll and admire nature's exhibition
By the soft light of the glowing moon.
Let me talk with you in confidence,
Embrace golden moment of pleasure,
And plan our course for an exciting future.

Nuptial Ablation ©

Oh, what a falling off there is,
A once sacred union built on cloud nine,
Conceived and committed to marital bliss,
A joint venture contracted for infinite time.
The time when two became a unit of one
What was jointly owned, is now "mine alone".

A union formed by exquisite love and romance,
Commitment to share "until death do us part",
Now starts a battle for control and dominance
The new idiom is "until love finds fault".
Insatiable desire invites temptation for dalliance,
Haplessly adulterating a once healthy rapport.

Marriage is usually predicated on dignity and trust.
Human, driven by greed and materialism,
Envisage a situation of infidelity and distrust.
The crystals, chattels, pets and home,
Are included into a pre-nuptial document.
What a falling off of compassion, love and respect.

Friendship and romance once riding high,
Destined for procreation and a loving home;
Are now, engaged in fracas, whimper, and sigh.
What should have been an easy solution
By choosing conference over confrontation,
Now left to the courts to decide the dissolution.

Ode to the Bed ©

The bed is our whole life my friend,
It is there we were likely conceived,
It is there some of us were born,
The bed is where we retire
To get a well-deserved siesta.

The bed is made of different materials,
Whether dried grass, dried leaves, or feathers.
It can be hard, firm, or soft,
By artisans who truly know their craft.
The bed is the origin and fall of nations.

The bed is where most people procreate
The place we fulfill our salacious desire.
The bed is where we meditate.
We return to it in life's autumn, to await the winter.
The bed is where most of us expire.

Once in a Lifetime ©

Once in a Lifetime you find that special person,
Your lives intermingle, and then you know
This is the beginning of all you yearn,
A love you can build on, a love that will grow.

I know for a fact, that miracle happens,
It happened to me, my dreams come true.
I know - I am that lucky person,
I have found that "Once in a lifetime" with you.

Your charm, humor and infectious smile,
Is truly beyond measure,
And as the mutual bond between us grew stronger,
I am grateful to have found a hidden treasure.

I loved you as a friend from the start,
Your beauty and brains captivated my soul
We fell in love, and I gave you my heart,
Today I give you my hand, and my love,
And more precious than gold - I give you my all.

Ode to a Dear Mother ©

The empty grey walls reflect her agony,
Void of the chatter and exuberance,
Where the children once sing and dance,
Now all grown and gone from mommy.
Gone from her nurturing guidance.

Her feeble frame wracked with pain.
Her head inclined to her feet
The once dancing legs are quiet
Fun, frolic and romance forever gone
When helpless infancy and old age repeat.

Her years of toil are now behind
She gropes her way in the darkness of age
Sweat beads from her wrinkled forehead
The window curtain closing out the world stage
As she nears the winter of human existence.

She stands and tries to reach out
She stumbles then she falls
She groans moans and sweats
She calls out for assistance
Timely she closes her eyes – she quits.

The Farmer Ants ©

There is an industrious ant specie
Known as 'philidris nagasau'
Living high in the trees of Fiji
In a parasitic plant called 'squamellaria'
Habitat for a very specialized ant community.

They use leaves as raft to cross streams,
Their bodies to build bridges or chain-gangs.
They construct dorms called 'domatium'
And culture their own fungi gardens
To establish their self-sustaining realm.

They exhibit superb hunting and farming ability
Spectacular teamwork it total unity.
Everyone – including sentries and janitors.
Any creature venturing into their territory.
Becomes fodder in their homey familial pantry.

Passport to Freedom ©

The time is fifteen minutes past eight
She waits to discuss their detachment
From their love enclave without a gate.
Mixed by feelings of ecstasy, and of doubt
Whether to request a hiatus, or just quit

Reluctantly she wants her autonomy,
Into a world she knows so well,
That is full of avarice and falsity,
Confused, but she would rather yield
Like a flightless bird into the wild.

The man is married and more mature,
A wife and three kids, plus two,
Yet she wants him in perpetuity.
He can endow her with exquisite luxury,
She can only satisfy his salacious fancy.

Cupid would then retract his arrow,
Replace the bow into its shield,
He will need it again someday, somehow
To shoot at another receptive burd
That may venture into his open field.

Evangelical Malfeasance ©

Hey high roller preacher man,
Have you heard the cries of hungry children?
Or those of the homeless population?
Perhaps not, over the din of your jet engine,
And living in a luxurious and palatial mansion.

The people are exhorted to give, and keep on giving,
From the paltry sum they earn for a living
While the Bible pages are the only thing you turn,
Because Pastor wants a mansion, or an airplane.
While the parishioners are on the brink of famine.

You extoll them to lift their voices and rejoice
Tithe to the max so you can get that Rolls Royce,
Bentley, or build a multi-million-dollar edifice
While some poor souls are destitute, and in pain.
How can you be a mediator between God and human?

Self-gratification becomes the key motivation;
Your pastoral office - an absolute mockery to salvation,
No nuance of humility, or what God's edicts should be.
No conscience, empathy, or sense of mediocrity
Just ultimate greed, exploiting the parishioners' idolatry.

Power of Words ©

The spoken word is like a shot fired,
Once it is spent, it is impossible to reclaim.
Words narrate history, events and legend,
Fact, fiction, and translate myriad of idioms.
They can shatter dreams, or energize them.

Words can abuse, calm, incite, and excite.
They can crush a heart, or heal it.
Can defame, demoralize, demean and denigrate.
Words express emotion, pleasure and pain,
It can educate, persuade, dissuade and impugn.

Words have double-meanings, and variations,
They can create obstacles, or mitigate them.
And can be manipulated and formulated to
Conform to any context, mood, or situation.
Avoid words that could debase your decorum.

Words are a powerful medium to communicate with,
Whether it's analog, digital, or cryptic.
They can obstruct connection, or facilitate it
People use words that are endearing and erotic,
To convey platonic and romantic sentience.
We have to use our words wisely.

Realization – Who Am I? ©

My heritage makes me strong.
My fears make me reluctant.
My selflessness makes me compassionate.
My confidence makes me competent.
My mistakes teach me to make good judgment.
My pride lifts my head high.
My courage to climb makes me victorious.
Perseverance empowers my quest for ideals.
My quest for knowledge sustains my mind.
My character makes me a wonderful person
If I cannot go on, that is not an option.
I do need Love and understanding.
My faith keeps me standing.
My spirituality makes me whole.
My insatiable essence makes me sensual.
I am human, and I am fallible.
But my integrity makes me honest.
Who am I?   I am a Libran,
Ken D the Cool Cat.

Photo by Ken Damally

Shelter of Love ©

Your love is a sheltering cove
Where I can evade my concern and anxiety.
I can feel the wind caressing my sentient body.
Knowing I can give my life and love willingly.
We are compatible, you make me very happy.

Your love is a sheltering arbor
Under which I can relax and brood.
We can listen to the birds chirping away,
Converse and share our philosophy
In ways we always understood.

Your love is my tower of strength,
I do not need to be apprehensive.
Your acceptance gives me extra certitude,
To conquer the world, feel and look good,
The dynamics to succeed.

Rain On Me ©

The once blue sky with patches of white cloud,
Quickly transform into ominous solid grey.
The wind dances and drifts across the land,
The gust intensifies, floating everything in its way.
I must seek shelter to escape nature's artistry.

The ferocious wind divests the verdant foliage,
The branches swayed by this unseen visitor,
With synchronized rhythm and barrage,
I contemplated nature's awesome power,
To rearrange or sustain all things under its sphere.

Just then another burst of light flashes overhead
Rain drops pelting my body and every canopy.
The wind caressing my cheek, my raiment doused,
Hail drops falling on every structure and vehicle.
The rhythmic precipitation makes you marvel.

The lightning flashes, the thunder rolls,
The whistling winds rattle the windows.
From my safe haven I listened to it all.
The heavens open its full might on the neighborhood.
Nature's marvelous power over humankind.

Courtesy www.picsearch.org

Speak to me of Love ©

When love beckons you, follow him,
Though the path may be hard and steep.
And when his wings enfold you, yield to him
Though the sword hidden among his pinions
May wound you.
And when he speaks to you believe in him,
Though his voice may shatter your dreams
As the north wind lays waste the garden.

As the cyclone, devastate the field,
So shall love make you stark naked.
Or grinds you with wind to whiteness.
Love will sustain growth and culture,
The essence for your peace and pleasure.

Love is self-sufficient and possesses not,
The main objective is to fulfill our desire
He'll knead you until you are pliant
Then assigns you to the sacred fire,
To be devoured in a sacred feast.

Adapted from "The Prophet" By Kahlil Gibran 1883-1931

Supplication ©

Please help me to understand your pain.
Help me to understand you, as a person.
Can we resurrect our marriage again?
Because of my sensitivity and fear,
It seems as if I did not care.

I was confused, and did not understand.
For the union to work, it takes two.
My true self I did not really discern.
Please help me to learn about you,
To reevaluate and start our life anew.

If there is any love left in your heart,
Save our marriage, don't let us part.
Please help me to move forward,
Leaving yesterday's baggage behind,
In order to rejuvenate the marital bond.

Sweet Surrender ©

Let me be the person to be your pillow,
To hold you in my arms complete,
I'll squeeze you gently, and make you smile
Ravage you with kisses sweet.
And to call you my sweetheart.

Let me kiss your cheeks, your lips, and hair,
I want to engage you in total splendor,
To explore your body with endless pleasure,
And sense the ecstasy of one absorbing kiss.
To steep my soul in eternal bliss.

Let me feel your amorous hands caress me tender
And smother me in the warmth of your embrace.
For your head, I will offer my shoulder
Cover me with the essence of your grace.
Until either of us surrender in romance.

The Diaper Man ©

Masquerading in his quirky apparel,
A man is searching for a party.
His peers stare in dismay,
While children laugh and jeer
At the unusual looking queer.

He means no harm to anyone,
Only wishes to create a flurry.
He asked of every child he sees,
None of them could ever declare,
Where the Masquerade Party is.

The cops and parents are flabbergasted,
And wondered who this dapper flasher is.
They decided to form a Pamper Patrol
To seek out this incredible prankster,
Then they discovered it is the Diaper Man.

Teatime ©

After hours of frenzied shopping,
It's three-thirty in the afternoon.
The bags are bearing me down,
I must take a pause downtown
A brief respite for teatime.

Above the incessant murmur of the patrons
Seated at cream linen-covered tables,
Teaspoons tinkle against china cups.
The waiter in black velvet tie rustles by
Serving delicious sandwiches on a silver tray.

Heavy velvet drapes, oak paneled cubicles,
Winged chairs, and overstuffed settees,
Clad in a hodgepodge of colorful designs.
The elegance of the décor so supreme,
Gives the ambiance of a luxurious living room.

My gastronomic breach is satiated,
The feet are reenergized, it's time to trod,
Leaving the tinkling, murmuring, gorging,
The aroma of myriad spices used for cooking;
Retreating from the ceremony of afternoon teatime.

The Canine and the Cock ©

In a quiet New Hampshire community,
A canine and a cock were neighbors.
The masters protected each other's property;
One with a canine, the other with a cock
But their charges were not so friendly
They listened each other across the fence,
And grew curious about each other's personality
But they were never introduced formally.

Due to a malfunction of the boundary
By misadventure, they eventually met
Curiosity quickly turn into disgust
The meeting grew hostile, and a brawl ensued.
The cock fought well, but the canine had the advantage.
When the dust settled, the canine killed the cock.
The canine maybe had in its mind,
He could get some cock soup for his master.

The cock's master sued for damages.
The canine went to court with his master, for defense
The Judge listened intently and adjudicated
The canine was guilty of homicide.
The Judge ordered that the canine be incarcerated,
Pending a sentence for the death penalty.
But the canine's sentence was later commuted
To that of exile from the neighborhood.
After which, the celebrity cock was buried.

Remodeling a Transgender ©

Need a little nip, tuck and butt enhancement,
For that special body part,
"Why not create some excitement?"
Come let me show you the latest in the art.

You'll not pay much for the consult,
But will be very pleased with the result.
When you sashay down the street,
There'll be admiration from all you meet and greet

People will certainly enquire,
Where you got that fabulous contour.
You'll appear foxy with your newly acquired figure,
Proud to show off your voluptuous, enhanced derriere.

There will be no adverse comment from admirers,
After treatment with a copious cocktail of a unique cement.
If you are too flat to trot, then you will get some fix-a-flat,
You can be sure the fix will be permanent.

You'll have a more corpulent derriere
With state-of-the-art procedure and utmost care.
With an unorthodox chemical brew including super glue,
You'll be almost brand new - a new and improved you.

You will get some mineral oil
That will also lubricate your joints and coil.
Then you can look like Jessica Rabbit,
When you consult Dr. Mel Surgeon, LGBT.

https://www.washingtonpost.com/news/morning-mix/wp/2017/03/28/woman-who-enhanced-butts-with-glue-and-cement-gets-10-years-for-manslaughter/?ref=yfp&utm_term=.c670b1e6f700

The Crow and the Pitcher ©

There is a crow, a certain kind of crow
That defies the term 'birdbrain'.
To see them improvise make you say, "Wow."
If you think you are smart, think again,
They are domiciled in New Zealand.

They are kid-smart as a six-year-old,
Use sticks to fetch food out of a nook.
They can make tools in the wild.
They use barbed leaf or wire for a hook
To access insects too far for their beaks.

Crows discern how objects react in water,
Drop in stones in water to raise the level,
To get at food in a water pitcher.
They are an amazingly smart creature
Perform feats that baffled many researchers.

Crows perform stealth operations on their own,
By stealing coins from a car-wash café.
They sneak through a coin basket slot,
To collect the coins like a thief.
That's when a camera caught the tricky culprit.

The Manhattan Crowd ©

Like assemblages of organisms darting back and forth
In vibrating ionic movement interrupted only by brief exchanges,
Jabbering, chattering in a thousand tones and languages.
Butting, greeting, aggregating and exchanging glances;
That is the daily routine of some in The Manhattan Crowd.

People constantly darting in, out, and roundabout hackney carriages,
Assorted automobiles appear as huge variegated bugs,
Humming, honking and belching toxic fumes.
Underground the earthshaking rattlers roll.
That is the motility of The Manhattan Crowd.

People of every status quo are sipping, nibbling and buying,
Street vendors occupy every space selling hot chestnuts, pretzels,
Hot dogs, corndogs, sodas, coffee, tea and bagels.
They're hoping you'll work up an appetite while browsing.
They are some of the traders in The Manhattan Crowd.

The budding stars, the mediocre, the talented and the boring,
Drumming, strumming, singing, signing and miming.
Provide drama to garner cash from the impromptu assembly,
They willingly perform for whatever the currency.
That's the outdoor arena for The Manhattan Crowd.

The glamorous, the debonair, brunettes, and men
Playing pocket billiard, locked in pelvic and derriere gaze, with lusting desires.
The primp women sashaying to display their voluptuous figures, while the charlatans, the pimps, the courtesans and the pick-pockets.
That's part of the assemblage of The Manhattan Crowd.

(**Manhattan Crowd** – Continued)

The beauties and the bums among the harried tourists,
The good, the bad, the ugly, and the miscreants,
The gamblers, the paraplegics, the sane and the insane;
Begging, crying, and yelping contemptuous invectives,
Those too comprise The Manhattan Crowd.

Humans puffing smoke like a diesel locomotive,
Rustling among the glitter, the glamour, the grime and crime.
The busybodies furtively seeking any unattended packages,
That could be his or her next gold mine.
That is the life of some in The Manhattan Crowd.

Daily the kinfolks converge in the concrete jungle;
CEOs, leaders, peons, Kings, Queens and squatters.
Some striving to surmount the economic struggle,
In this magnificent metropolis which will oblige,
Everyone included in the Manhattan Crowd.

The skirted, the suited, the semi-nude and villains,
The militants, the gangsters all babbling and cackling,
Bartering, meeting, touching, chatting, and cursing,
Some possess varying level of proficiency and learning.
They make up part of The Manhattan Crowd.

The early Dutch settlers bought Manhattan Island from Indians for twenty-four ($24.00) dollars in 1626.
They paid four thousand eight hundred ($4,800.00) dollars for Brooklyn which the Indians valued higher because it was good farm land.
Manhattan became one of the greatest cultural, commercial and financial centers of the world.
Central Park consists of 843 acres and the most visited urban park in the nation.
Ripley's – Believe it or Not

The Recluse ©

I am trying hard to comprehend,
Please help me to understand.
I know I have a pulsing heart,
But no relationship with even a rodent.

I have no asset, not even a cookie jar.
I do not make love, nor war.
I do not work, play, or interact with others,
Don't even know if I have relatives.

People in the metropolis are quite busy,
I am moving, just as others around me.
I can hear every automobile engine,
But I have no sense of musical rhythm.

I must be a misfit amid opulence and luxury,
Or a freak of nature in a quandary.
Maybe just a living organism of sorts
Occupying a tiny space of the universe

The Rattler ©

The monstrous creature rumbles under the borough,
Meandering through tunnels and over bridges.
Its stomach gorged with a cargo of gems and myrrh,
Occasionally stopping to excrete and devour.

Wherever it trod, the earth and buildings shake.
It hisses, rattles, and shrieks, as it rumbles on
In its graffiti skin, layered with grime,
Throughout the city that is always awake.

The mechanical creature burrows into the tunnels,
Under land or sea and out again
Screeching, rattling and hissing as it rumbles,
Clothed in its shiny or multi-colored skin.

Occasionally, people are caught in its steely grip,
Commuters thrown in all directions.
After a screeching halt, the victim is a lifeless heap,
There can be silence, or a painful groan.

Uptown, Downtown, across town, or in between,
The Rattler conveys people at quickened pace twenty-four seven.
Connecting Burroughs, Cities, Counties, or States,
That is the mission of New York's Subway system.

THE SPANISH NEEDLE

Lovely dainty Spanish needle
With your yellow flower and white,
Dew bedecked and softly sleeping,
　Do you think of me to-night?
Shadowed by the spreading mango,
Nodding o'er the rippling stream,
Tell me, dear plant of my childhood,
　Do you of the exile dream?
Do you see me by the brook's side
Catching crayfish 'neath the stone,
As you did the day you whispered:
Leave the harmless dears alone?
Do you see me in the meadow
coming from the woodland spring
with a bamboo on my shoulder
　And a pail slung from a string?
Do you see me all expectant
　lying in an orange grove,
while the swee-swees sing above me,
　waiting for my elf-eyed love?
Lovely dainty Spanish needle,
Source to me of sweet delight,
In your far-off sunny southland
　Do you dream of me to-night?

～Claude McKay

The Soldier Boy ©

Between early childhood and adulthood,
We find the military recruits in training,
On the hills of the Blue Mountain region.
They're now on the threshold of manhood,
To become a protector of the nation.

They come in assorted sizes and statures,
Strutting their stuff before drill instructors.
They are sly as a fox, lazy as a sloth,
The energy of a snail, and brains of an idiot,
Hoping they find another recruit to outsmart.

They dislike reveille, and physical training,
Donning the uniform, or being on parade.
Abhors cleaning their dirty barrack rooms,
And the harsh, rugged, jungle exercise in the field.
But they accept the government supporting them.

Their interests are girls, sprees, skirts and movie.
They have an uncanny ability to lie like a sailor.
They possess the inspiration of a Casanova.
A soldier is a magical creature in uniform,

Difficult for any woman to avoid his charisma.

The Toiler's Agony ©

Like the lone picture hanging on the wall,
Essie stood in the sparsely furnished room,
Staring at the termite infested den.
They once absorbed the sounds of laughter,
But now, all the children except one, is gone.

Essie was once a woman full of grace,
She and Gus travelled wide for adventure,
He is long gone, but she is stuck in one place.
No more wonderful moments of pleasure
Her feet is drawing nearer to her face.

Left alone to face the world in solitude,
She stood by the wooden louver window to read.
Her body is wracked by aches and pains,
Her groans and moans fill the cabin
Just hobbling along until life's end.

__Positive Attitudes__ ©

Be educated in order to be elevated,
Learning is a very sacred endeavor.
Always be ethical so you can be trusted
Because politeness attracts and sustains favor.

Anger destroys the person, so have a sense of humor.
Decency is far more valued than obscenity.
Give yourself credit for positive endeavors,
A smile will always enhance your personality.

Count your blessings every day,
Do not let disappointments get you down.
Rejuvenate, act like a child, and take time to play
A cheerful heart will always stay young.

People will gravitate to empathy and integrity,
Avoid preoccupation with the self, or falsity,
Refresh the soul with endearing spirituality.
Exercise the body and mind for prolonged longevity.

Engage whatever is meaningful and wholesome,
Think, plan, and explore them.
Without laws, wise men would live the same.
If you are happy, then you have wealth and fame.

Courtesy www.picsearch.org

Love Quest ©

Wanted! Someone who is natural and caring,
Not keen on materialism, or to gain the universe.
One who is personable, and a zest for living
Not wanting a palatial life of opulence
One who desires bliss, humility, and with poise.

Wanted! A person whom I can trust with my fantasies,
Kind, intelligent, loving, sentient, and receptive.
A sense of humor, and have pleasant discourse.
With elegance that floats with grace and love.
One with fine attributes and exuberance.

Wanted! One who can make my life complete,
To achieve our common goals and pursuit
Someone attentive, and in whom I can confide.
Characteristics and modesty most compatible
That special person who can electrify my world.

Courtesy www.picsearch.org

Together In Love ©

When we are close together,
We differ only as individuals.
We are together in love and aspirations,
In our activities, spirit, and divine embrace
We are in a devoted union of permanence.

When we are close together
We share common interests and values.
Engage in our simple sensual splendor,
Hear our hearts measured beat,
In the splendor of our love and trust.

When we are close together,
The world around us seems perfect.
We share good times and hearty laughter
Because our friendship evolved from the heart
Let's embrace and pledge our love forever.

Photo by Ken Damally

Tropical Treasure ©

Washed by the diaphanous waters of the Caribbean,
Formed by a mix of fine white sands,
Baked by the tropical sun,
Cooled by the invigorating trade winds,
Come and bask on the beaches in my hometown.

Raft on the Rio Grande or Martha Brae,
And wine, dine and dance at elegant cafes.
Rejuvenate at a mineral spring, or a waterfall,
Or just listen to pulsating reggae rhythms.
It's an adventure in fun, romance, and repose.

Look up to the majestic mountain ranges,
Flush with exotic fruits in abundance.
Avocados, mangoes, tangerine and oranges.
Coffee, cocoa, coconut, nutmeg and apples.
The land of love "Out of many, one people".

Courtesy www.picsearch.org

Twilight Time ©

As the night gently spread its canopy
And jealously obscure the sultry day,
Out comes the winged creatures of the night.
As the diurnal ones stealthily depart,
From an active day, to rest in the moonlight.

The moon emerges over the mountain,
Bathing terra firma with its soft silvery beam.
The river flows through the lush glen,
Moonlight reflection rippling off the stream,
Rushing to meet the sea for a mating waltz.

The stars glitter in the distant skies,
Fusing with the moonlight for a welcome.
Then appear the cicadas and the fireflies,
The invisible wind rustles the fragrant jasmine,
Ah! Nature's therapy for meditation and diversion.

The Galeon 1513

What is Mankind? ©

Mankind was given the gift of life from unseen hands
Into a world full of strife and turmoil.
We gather and disperse our families and friends
Like an overused paper towel,
But some people never envisage returning to the soil.

Mankind is like a flower that blooms in the morning
Exuding beauty and sweet fragrance,
Garnering the most exquisite opulence,
Then fading into obscurity in the evening,
Leaving no trace of their existence.

Mankind violates the rules of our existence,
Not cognizant that cavitation can follow ascension.
Congruent to the four seasons of the year,
So is the transition of every life in the universe.
Honesty, integrity and ethics of excellence is stellar.

Wake Up People ©

Wake up everybody! Men, women and children
Create a firm foundation based on education,
Seek knowledge and dispel hypocrisy.
Be proud of your ancestral admonition
To lift up your heads high and practice civility.

You complain about racial inequality,
But continue to whittle away your money
Not for an education, but hoarding gadgetry.
High time to reject the degenerative proclivity
And try to mitigate the ethnic disparity.

Restore confidence and wisdom to a powerful mind,
Cultivate positive thoughts and vibrations.
Keep your communities free from derision,
It's a covert plan for failure and stagnation,
By eroding the last bit of hope and ambition.

Strive for academic and economic parity,
Show respect for your commune and family,
Stop inflicting pain, and emasculating your race.
Inculcate dignity, empathy, and humanity,
To rejuvenate the smile that dissipated from your face.

When Will We Learn? ©

When will we learn that killers and miscreants?
Aren't governed by our laws, or care to be civil.
That we retract muscle, power, and strength
From the law officers and good citizens,
And give license to those that commit evil?

When will the governance recognize its obligation,
By protecting law-abiding citizens and assuring
Peace, life, liberty, justice, and prosperity.
When does everyone recognize the cost to the nation?
Of the anarchy and debauchery, that enervates the society?

When do we assess the costs of mediocrity?
The chagrin of productive citizens,
The plague of death, destruction, rape, robbery.
The demise of communities and civic amenities?
A failure in polity to enforce the laws of civility.

Why not put killers away permanently,
Those who take lives simply because it is easy?
They find such adventure, kicks and thrill,
And keep getting away with it - absolutely.
Some are caught, caged and bailed - to continue kill.

How do we feel when our beloved family,
Mothers, and young children are executed?
Productive citizens become victims of barbarity.
Entrepreneurs and taxpayers are decimated
When we all pay for crime in dollars and death

Ode To a Dad ©

A Dad is all about sensibility and nurture,
He gives his children reasons to be proud.
A father is biological, a purpose of nature,
Some sincere, others deceptive and wayward.

A Dad is strong in faith, courage and conviction,
And very sensitive to his family's need.
He is always around to fulfill his obligation,
And gives his presence, helping them to succeed.

A Dad accepts children as they are,
Genuinely appreciates their unique qualities.
He shows everyone how to care,
And not perturbed about their worldly frailties.

Every child needs a Dad who loves unconditionally,
Who teach them how to win, to lose, and be polite.
He expresses self-confidence in wisdom and ability,
Committing always do what is right.

A Dad finds the bright side of a difficult situation,
Shows children the benefits of new experience.
He knows perspective can influence perception,
So, he sets reasonable goals and exercise patience.

A Dad does not encourage materialism,
He encourages high ideals, and of being a leader.
A Dad extols high ideals and great enthusiasm,
He is a coach, a friend, a mentor and supporter.

A Dad should be fun to be around,
The person children look up to and adore.
Someone everyone loves to the ground,
Who narrates stories, tell jokes, and much more.

A Good Mother ©

A mother is very special with a caring heart.
Who make great sacrifices for her family,
A Role model, guardian, and nurturer
Provides clothes, food and security
A mother gives all these things and more
Giving encouragement when skies are grey.

A mother is very loving with the sweetest word,
Able, ready, and willing to lend a hand
To smooth things out a little when they don't go as planned.
Someone dearly loved, and that is surely true
When others lose their faith in you,
That is just when hers will start.

She is naturally a matriarch of the family
Her love is a sheltering tree
Providing emotional comfort with humility
So that the homestead stays in harmony
A haven of peace, love and serenity
For the benefit of everybody.

Her integrity ripples through the generations
Trying to make this world a better niche.
Oftentimes emotionally and physically stressed
Sometimes disrespected and abused
But without mothers to perpetuate life
This earth would have been a desolate place.

Winter Winds ©

The wicked winter winds whip across the Hudson,
Zero temperature, no heat in the building.
Cheeks, heads, fingers, and toes freezing,
Everyone seeks comfort and warming,
To avoid the frigid wind howling and whistling.

The oil-fired burner is old and broken,
No telling when repairs will be done.
The frosty windows need replacement,
Placing every resident in severe plight.
Such is life on a New York winter night.

The assemblage of people is always scrambling,
Dashing into public transport or any building.
The homeless are cursing and grumbling,
At the snowflakes dousing their fires,
Some boozers lying in melted slush.

The once verdant Central Park in summer,
The placid lake, and beautiful flora,
Now experience the worst kind of weather,
All blanketed with the snowflakes of winter.
But for me - my body refuses to surrender.

Yearning ©

My eyes yearn to see,
Young people embrace positive attitudes,
Assisting and encouraging their peerage.
To undertake meaningful projects of merit
That is worthy of the greatest homage.

My ears yearn to hear,
Kind words of admiration and gratitude.
Expressions of love, laughter and exultation,
Engulfing every man, woman and child.
Because we are all God's children.

My heart yearns to know,
That someday the unrelenting suffering,
Will transform into goodwill, dignity and leniency.
No one is an island, we should exhibit unity,
Embrace hope, love, and peace for all humanity.

My eyes, my ears, and my heart are weary,
To witness the wanton disregard for life,
Personal, public, or private property.
The bawdiness, crudeness, lewdness and rudeness
That permeates almost every community.

Young People's Creed ©

Your presence is a gift to the world,
You came here for a purpose.
You are unique, and one of a kind,
Engage your mind to find your goal.
You can be what you want to be - just be bold.

Count your blessings, not your troubles or setbacks,
Do not harbor useless regrets or borrow trouble.
Do the best you can, push ahead, and stay on track,
And avoid negative and unhappy people.
Develop courage, be strong, and be ethical.

Do not impose limits on your ability, or self
Your dreams are waiting to take flight.
Do not leave your important goals to chance,
Your goals, your prize, are at the summit.
Shape the path you wish to traverse.

Imaginary things waste more energy than real ones,
Learn and look for pleasure in little things.
The longer a problem is carried, the heavier it gets.
Do not take yourself too seriously- have fun,
Live a life of serenity, not a life regret.

Devotion ©

I Love you,
As from my heart, I say the words,
I hear it in the songs of birds,
I Love you.

I Love you,
My heartbeats gaily pound your name,
And through the summer just the same
I Love you

I Love you,
A thousand springs will brightly say,
Never less ardent than today,
I Love you.

I Love you,
Every morsel I tried to nibble on
You are constantly on my mind
I Love you.

I Love you,
Every waking moment my thoughts on you
Almost every dream converges on you too
I Love you.

I Love you,
As the years, go swiftly by,
I know I'll love you till I die,
I Love you.

Meaning of Life ©

Humanity greatest need is to find the meaning of life
It may be difficult to explain or to grasp, but it endures.
We need positive challenges, not strife,
However, we should not be afraid to explore.
But just to find a meaning to live life.

Listen, discover, and develop ethical practices
To shape the path, we will traverse.
Ponder our relationship with the universe,
And pursue dreams for a larger purpose.
Find a person to love and have discourse.

We cannot invent a meaning for our life
To survive our affluent air-conditioned society,
Where humankind is pampered and spoiled,
By the softness of modern computerized culture,
Where dynamic technologies replace common sense.

Courtesy www.picsearch.org

Dancing in Lovers' Cove ©

Once in a lifetime you find someone special,
Your lives intermingle,
The touch of a hand, and a warm welcoming smile.
And you feel the sense of belonging in friendship,
And you notice it after a while in the sound of a voice,
Somehow you realize this is what you have longed for,
An affection you can build on, a love that will grow--
A miracle happens, and dreams all come true—
As our heart-to-heart talks start to show.

One of life's nicest gifts is a genuine friend
A person who can make us laugh,
And lift our spirits in a way no one else can.
A faithful friend who is a sure shelter,
With deep understanding that both can share,
A gift of love that is destined to mature.
Whoever finds one has found a treasure
A faithful friend is something beyond price
There's no measuring of their worth.

Courtesy www.picsearch.org

The Unforgettable Woman ©

The woman a man remembers is indeed unique,
Enabling a life changing experience
The one who can give him security.
She is the one who can offer him solace,
And fruitful encounter by her sensuality.

The more a woman seeks to live naturally,
She can be gentler she is in her judgments.
And manifest her love emotionally and spiritually,
The more brilliant her inward virtue shows
Thus, radiating outwardly for the world to see.

The woman who exhibits elegance and grace,
Producing a man his first offspring
The more she'll be the woman of choice
The woman who is caring and nurturing,
Is most likely to be - the unforgettable woman.

The Back Nine - The Dash of Life ©

Today is the first day of the rest of your life,
It is the oldest you've ever been,
And the youngest you'll ever be hereafter.
"Life" is a gift to us all, defined by a "DASH"
Recognize your lifespan is like the four seasons
Spring, summer, autumn and winter.

Life is not the materialism you gather,
Like automobiles, jewelry, or a mansion.
Your health is the real wealth – not cash.
It is the good deeds and seeds you scatter,
Exemplify the life you lived between the **DASH**.
Make it your gift to those who come after.

Experience comes from making bad judgments;
Good judgment evolves out of experience,
But it serves to make us stronger and wiser,
Some people are not so privileged
So be grateful for your accomplishments
Their "dash" has already been utilized.

As we enter the autumn and winter seasons
Our brain, ears, eyes, and joints begin to wane
With diminished strength and agility
When the aches and pains begin,
Diminished physical and mental acuity.
Once an adult, and then a child again.

During the seasons, inculcate the seeds of ambition.
Let your mouth speak words of kindness and wisdom,
Uphold integrity and live a life of dignity.
Make the DASH of life a fantastic one.
Strive for prosperity, but live ethically.
LIVE, LAUGH, LOVE, and LEARN every day.

CONGRATULATIONS

GRADUATION

Go forward
Ready to
Accept life's challenges
Determined to learn and
Understand,
Alert to, and avoid
Temptations, lust, and greed.
Interested in yourself,
Others, and
Never forgetting that "No one is an Island".

• •

Dreams are life seeds of achievement.
Plant them in the richness of your experience.
Tend to them with perseverance.
Guard the tender shoots from self-doubt,
And one day, your dreams will no longer
Be your dreams, but your realities.
You can be anything you want to be,
It's all up to you, and no one else.
I wish you the joy of purposeful life.
I wish you new worlds and the vision to see them.
I wish you the decency and nobility of which you're capable.

Courtesy www.picsearch.org

Affirmation of Life ©

Live your wonderful life to the fullest,
Never harbor any fear or doubt.
In everything give your utmost best,
The benefits will one day manifest.

Never be afraid to leave the beaten path,
Persist until you ultimately succeed.
Think positively and have steadfast faith,
And reevaluate your feats as you proceed.

You can achieve whatever you attempt,
Have the courage to take on the task at hand.
Even if you're void of a bed, food, or a cent,
Appreciation and humility will pay dividend.

Garden of Love

Spice of Life ©

Open your garden of myrrh and love potion
With respect, gratitude and adulation.
Laugh, love, play and embrace often.
Talk and touch lovingly and sensually.
Show and tell of your aspirations.

Love live and grow in its freedom,
If there's compatibility and empathy.
Let the child within emerge, to reduce tension
Explore new and novel ideas of romance,
And make time to be alone for meditation.

Practice the art of complimentary seduction,
To bring creativity to the relationship.
Affirm, support, and trust each other
Show compassion, grace and patience.
Develop and foster healthy independence.

Girl from Ipanema (*Reprise*)

What a beautiful woman full of grace
A body tanned by the Ipanema sun
Exuding a perfect captivating radiance
The sway in her hips is more than a poem
She's the most elegant woman to be seen.
Like an angel sent down from heaven.

Seductive, tall, tanned, young and lovely
The girl from Ipanema goes walking by
Her hips swing so cool and sways so gently
They gyrate with such rhythm like a samba
Each time she passes to Ipanema playa
He would just give his heart willingly.

Oh, why am I so lonely and moody?
When such beauty exists, which isn't mine
If only she knew when she passes by
My whole world is filled with love divine
She seems more beautiful every passing day.
But she just looks straight ahead and not at him.

By Antonio Carlos Jobim (1962)

The Girl from Ipanema" ("Garota de Ipanema") written in 1962 by Antonio Carlos Jobim with lyrics in Portuguese by Vinicius de Moraes and in English by Norman Gimbel was recorded by Astrud Gilberto, João Gilberto and Stan Getz, in March 1963 as part of the album Getz/Gilberto, released March 1964

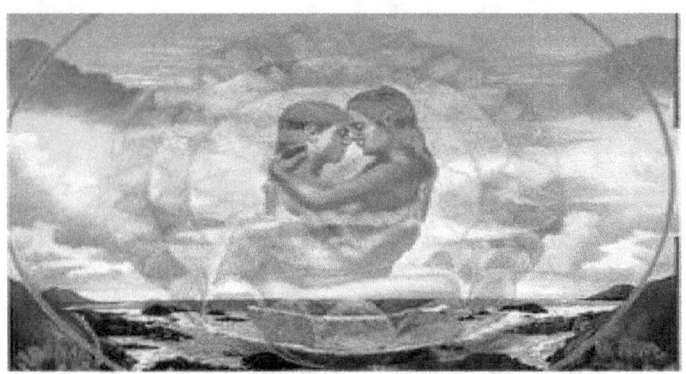
Courtesy www.picsearch.org

Soul Mate ©

It was an August morning in twenty-ten
A new chapter of my life began.
On scenic Sterling Castle height,
In my beautiful Jamaican hometown
I found my gorgeous soul mate.

What a joy to wake up at morning's light
To see the dawn, and then the rising sun.
The crisp wind blows through the louver,
I welcomed the sun's invigorating ray,
And let the mountain breeze caress my body.

The crowing roosters welcome the new day.
I prayed for health and longevity,
Buoyed by my soul mate's erogeneity.
I gave thanks for a lover and a friend
And pledge my unconditional devotion.

If you are alone, I will be your shadow,
If you want to cry, I will offer my shoulder
If you want a hug, I will be your pillow
If you need to be happy, I will make you smile
Anything you need as friend, just give me a call.

Courtesy www.picsearch.org

Protect our Children ©

All things bright and beautiful,
All creatures great and small
All things wise and wonderful
The Creator made them all.

Children are the most precious gift,
The world awaits their eager young minds.
They are adventurers, explorers, and keen sleuths,
Protect them from dangerous conditions.

Birds can fly, the children will not,
Fish can swim, most children cannot.
Children move and work very fast,
So does chemicals, poisons and toxins.

Safety has no quitting time
Prevention is better than cure
Practice safety all the time
Safety makes sense, it's best for everyone.

Courtesy www.picsearch.org

The Young Child ©

Childhood is a period of transitioning,
And the child possesses a surprising memory.
A young child is constantly learning,
But they are unable to articulate clearly.

The child likes to pretend and imagine,
Fostering wishes and great expectations.
The young child needs love and affection,
The adult's presence, not their presents.

The child holds strong belief, but need supervision,
The closeness of caring and nurturing parents.
The young child feels the world of dissension,
But the child is unable to pacify conflicts.

The young child has seeds of greatness,
And sprout like a beautiful flower.
The child can manifest itself in myriad of ways,
They speak the language of their own culture.

Hair ©

Like the herbage that bedeck terra firma,
The fur that clothes most animals,
The scales that adorn most marine life,
Humans wear their crowning glory
In diverse colors and array.

The faddist and the fashionable,
The cultist and the freaky hold sway.
People's belief and taste come in play,
In coiffures that defy modesty
To get a few moments of idolatry.

The dreadlocks, braid, Mohawks and Afro
Everyone to their own style and fashion
The Rasta, hippy, clown and courtesan
Wear a style to fit their every occasion
Staking their claim on self-expression.

The hairdresser or the tonsorial artisan
Transform the kinky or the short mane,
The bald, the beautiful, the flamboyant
The soft, curly, fuzzy, or straight hair;
Into an excellent work of art.

"Pleasing the eyes of other people are the eyes that ruin us.
Any person who adorns them self to suit everybody - will soon whittle away.
They crave fine clothes, houses, furniture, body contour, skin tone, and jewelry.
To satisfy the inquisitive eyes of others - to their own detriment."
A lone flower still blossoms for its own purpose – not for admirers.   – Ken Damally

Soul Devotion ©

A new chapter of our life has begun
New endeavors and new mission,
Renewed commitment and vision
Individual goals coordinated
Doing things and going places in unison.

As our relationship thrives and matures,
We will explore our amorous sides
To experience a rebirth of devoted bliss.
We will engage in kind words and deeds,
And espouse every moment to cherish.

As we are discovering our new beginnings,
To grow and nurture our commitment,
Explore adventure, excitement, and leisure
Dismiss all negative thoughts and distractions
Embrace living, loving and pleasure.

The Life of Grass ©

Entranced by the verdant raiment of mother earth
Its omniscient beauty adorns the environs
Of celebrities, royalties, peons and the wealthy
Manicured into the most attractive landscapes
The alluring beauty extolled in books and songs.

It is groomed, nurtured, and sometimes replicated
Then trudged on, spat on, and defecated on
Manipulated by animals, man and machines
Even Mother Nature mete out arid abuse
Yet it rebounds with amazing resilience.

It sacrifices its life to sustain the lives of others
By providing fodder, clean the atmosphere
And help to regulate the earth's temperature.
Even after its demise in myriad of ways
It's fragmented for bedding, feed and mulch.

Grass at times deemed invasive and a nuisance
But the tranquil verdant charm offers solace
Human enjoy the texture for romantic splendor
As it forms a canopy for the final resting place
Magnificent terrains in splendid greenery.

The glory of man is as the flower of grass
As the grass withers, the flower lapse.
All creatures in the flesh is as the grass
Regardless of color, creed, or caste
Everything on earth is like the four seasons.

Ras Tafari ©

There goes the Rasta man
Skanking like a dragon
Wearing sandals as if he's a centurion
Dazzling white teeth, just like pearls
Flashing eyes like those of a lemur.

There goes the Rasta man
With each stealthy step like a lion
Not creating any problem
Or plotting any nefarious schism
Because he's a real true Brethren.

There goes the Nyabinghi man
Puffing the chillum like a coal train
Trotting as if going to Jah Kingdom
Hailing every Brethren and Sistren
In honor of Ras Tafari Makonnen.

Jamaica is not just about reggae!
Rastafarianism is also a religion
Long beards, and dreadlocks like Medusa
Speak the most unique idiom, and use ganja
But an affable and distinctive Rasta.

Rastafarian evolved from the name Ras Tafari Makonnen (1892–1975) who was crowned Emperor Haile Selassie I (1930–1974) on November 2, 1930 as Emperor of Ethiopia. Makonnen assumed as his imperial name and titles Haile Selassie I, King of Kings, Lord of Lords, Conquering Lion of the Tribe of Judah, Elect of God, and Light of the World, deemed as a politico-religious redeemer. Rastafarianism evolved from the religious tenets as perceived by his followers.
*In what was one of the first countries to adopt Christianity, the **Makonnens** had long before claimed descent from the biblical Judaic king, Solomon, and Candace, the queen of Sheba.*

Jamaica sunset

Eventide Aura ©

The calm of the twilight and the gentle wind
Create whispers among the trees as they stood
Hushed on tiptoe, for the sight of the moon.
The soft petals of the flora voluntarily fold
To hide their stamens after a day of incursions.

As the night falls and the wind and waves lull
I watched the interplay of the moonlight
With the shadow reflecting on the wavelets.
As each passing cloud gently roll on by
Showing an array of magical sparkles.

Out on the water could be seen the reflection
Of the trees bending to admire their profiles
As the wind wrinkles the surface of the lake,
A fish leaps out of the water to get its canape
On a gnat skimming the surface for a drink.

The soft summer breeze wraps itself around me
Caressing my body with a graceful rhythm
As the afternoon raindrops fell in gentle squalls
Over the garden and verdant shrubs around,
Reviving them from the stupor of the sun's steam.

Liberation of Life ©

Live this wonderful life to the fullest,
Spend time with positive people who are smart
We can achieve whatever we attempt,
By relinquishing any apprehension or doubt.
Never be afraid to leave the beaten path,
Muster the courage to take on the task at hand.
And reevaluate the results as you proceed.

In everything give the ultimate best,
The benefits will one day manifest.
Have a self you love and respect
Think positively and have steadfast faith,
Persist until you ultimately succeed.
Even if you're void of a bed, food, or a cent
Gratitude and humility indeed pay dividend.

Engage people who reflect positive personality,
People to admire, love and respect,
Show candor, courage, and mental acuity
Relationships should enhance - not hurt
Emancipate yourself from negative people.
Embrace compassion and civility
To live and experience personal fulfillment.

Turn all disappointments into strength
To enjoy life's process, not just the rewards
Coalesce with conscientious family and friends
And be proud to be a part of the big picture.
Commit to and embrace the spirit of excellence
Surround yourself with happy people,
To produce the desired benefits to your life.

Falling in Love ©

Falling in love with you is something
I would replicate over and over.
When you smile and reach for my hand
The same breathless feeling recurs
Then I know that I want to spend
The rest of my life endlessly loving you.

Love is like a garden of roses always blooming
Where the sun is always shining,
The fragrance of a thousand blossoms,
The beauty of knowing you're near
Where the season is always spring.
I found a world of happiness here.

I can always sense your gentle kindness,
That exemplifies care and understanding
It warms my heart when I see your face
The feeling of closeness and comfort
Completely, in the circle of your embrace
Our special love is all I think about.

I found a world of beauty in you
A world of solace that I always knew
There's someone out there for me,
Who cares, and make me feel anew
Thank God the day that I found you
I knew all my dreams would come true.

Our Journey of Life ©

Life is like a journey on a train with its stations, change of routes, and accidents!

At birth we boarded the train and met our parents who bought the tickets,

We believe they will always travel on this train by our side.

However, at some station our parents will step down from the train, leaving us on this journey alone.

As time goes by, other passengers will board the train, many of whom will be significant:

Our siblings, friends, children, and even the love of our life.
Many will step down and leave a permanent vacuum in our lives.

Others will go so unnoticed that we won't even know when they vacated their seats and got off the train!
This train ride will be full of joy, sorrow, fantasy, expectations, hellos, good-byes, and farewells.
A successful journey is having a good relationship with all passengers...

Making sure that we give our best to make their journey comfortable.
The mystery of this fabulous journey is:
We do not know at which station we ourselves will step down so, we must live in the best way - adjust, forget, forgive, love and offer the best of who we are.

It is important to do this because when the time comes for us to leave our seat empty...

We should leave behind beautiful memories for those who will continue to travel on the "train of life."
I wish you a joyful journey on the train of life.
Reap success and give lots of love.
More importantly, thank God for the journey.

I don't know when my station will come... don't want to miss saying:
"Thank you for being one of the passengers on my train."
Again, I thank you

Wasted Lives ©

Standing under the bodega lights of Eastside
Are the street crazies and druggies
Wretched souls darting everywhere
Boozing, snorting, and playing pocket billiards
Swearing at anyone who dare to stare.

The smell of ganja wafting in the wind
Boom box blaring the latest hip-hop tunes
All night long - disturbing the neighborhood
Sirens of ambulances, fire trucks and police
Constantly blaring throughout the hood.

Beggars in grimy tattered rags
Roam the streets or ride the trains
Cadging for a hand-out, or a ration
Others roll the dice for a quick fix
Obscenities venting from their wobbly casing.

Deep in the alleyways, or under a stoop
Dry or wet in the sweltering heat
Homeless men are obliged to sleep,
Bag ladies ride the trains at night;
Their worldly wares in sacks or carts.

Avoid anything that is easy.
What comes Easy won't Last
What Lasts won't come Easy.

The Beauty of a Good Wife ©

Happy is the husband of a really good wife;
With a cheerful of face, whatever the season
He will have a long and peaceful life
The amiable wife is the joy of her husband
An earthly angel sent from heaven.

A good wife is the best of portfolios
Invested in by the Bonds of Marriage
Reserved for the gentleman who avows
That rich or poor, they'll be glad at heart
But he is also responsible for the maintenance.

The grace of a wife will charm her husband
Her accomplishments make him stronger
Like the sun rising over the mountain
She'll be that joy in the morning
To light the world with her softer glow.

A modest wife is really a treasure
To be shown gratitude and kindness
She needs confirmation of her power
Her chaste character is beyond measure
Always striving to make the family better.

Qualities of a Beautiful Woman.

With those attractive lips - speak words of geniality.
Use those lovely eyes to seek out the good in people.
To maintain that gorgeous slim figure, share your food with the hungry.
Your beautiful hair, let a child run his/her fingers through it once a day.
For poise, walk with the knowledge that you never walk alone.
People, even more than things, have to be restored, renewed,
Revived, reclaimed, and redeemed - never disregard anyone.
Remember, if you ever need a helping hand,
You will find one at the end of each of your arms.
As you grow older, you will discover that you have two hands;
One for helping yourself, and the other for helping others.

Audrey Hepburn

The Power of a Woman ©

A real woman is a man's best friend.
She will never stand him up and never let him down.
She will reassure him when he feels insecure
And will always comfort him after a bad day.
She will inspire him to do things he never thought
He could do - and to live without fear.

She will enable him to express his deepest emotions
And give in to his most intimate desires.
She will make sure he always feels as though he's
The most handsome man and will enable him
to be most confident, sexy, seductive and invincible
By expressing words of love and pleasantries.

She in turn needs confirmation of her power,
So never forget to let her know that you truly love her
Give affection, Pay attention, and Show appreciation
Or she may succumb to the natural temptation
And try out her feminine power on another man
Resulting in the dissolution of the union.

Monkey See - Monkey Sue ©

A curious crested-macaque named Naruto
Inadvertently became a celebrity photographer
Living somewhere in a British zoo
He can snap a perfectly framed selfie
Gaining the dubious title of an 'author'.

The curious monkey with a toothy grin
Develop a knack with the camera button
But due to inane human intervention
Naruto became the subject of litigation
Brought on by people across the Pond.

An American group called PETA
Sued in the defense of Naruto
To protect the copyright of the simian photo
Totally unaware of all the ruckus
That human could be so frivolous.

The case of an ape in another country
Was in the 9th Circuit Court of Frisco.
Observed by citizens and law students
Even the judges chuckled at the novelty
Often bursting out in loud laughter.

The litigators claim to have a relationship
To represent the monkey in court
In order to protect his 'authorship'.
But did they really care one iota
Or just a ruse for their own profit?

Adapted from:
www.apnews.com/4d29899e23ba41f4bd0149885ecf01a7/No-monkeying-around:-Court-weighs-if-animal-owns-its-selfies
Written by: Linda Wang

Island of Love – Jamaica ©

When the sun finally sets over the horizon,
And the night spread its wings over the land,
I watched the moon rises over the Blue Mountains,
Shedding its soft silvery light over the lush terrain.

Down in the valley the Rio Grande dances and roams,
With a whisper under the seductive moon beams,
The glistening water rushes to the mighty ocean
Carrying fresh mineral water from the mountains.

The tranquility of the twilight is occasionally broken
By nightingales singing a farewell lullaby
Or the distant laughter of children, or a swain,
Signaling the close of another hectic day.

The weary children are home from classes
Homework done; evening chores completed
Prayers said, sweet dreams and goodnight kisses
Very soon every kinfolk will be tucked in bed.

Meaning of Life ©

Human undying quest is to find the meaning of life
It may be difficult to explain or to grasp, but for sure.
We need positive challenges, not strife,
Gather courage and not be afraid to explore.
And find a positive meaning to live life.

Listen, discover, and develop ethical customs
To shape the path, we will traverse.
Ponder our relationship with the universe,
And pursue dreams for a larger purpose.
Then find people to love and have a discourse.

We cannot invent a meaning for our lives
To survive our affluent air-conditioned society.
Where humankind is pampered and become loutish,
By the softness of modern electronic gadgetry,
Where dynamic technologies replace common sense.

Midnight Kiss ©

As the midnight hour approaches on New Year's Eve
Everyone gathers to ring in the festive affair
Family, friends and strangers falling in love
Having exuberant chatter and laughter
While the jazz band played with increasing tempo
In the background some watched the TV.

The clock ticks away the minutes and seconds
Elsewhere myriad of people gathered in Times Square
Here at the venue champagne glasses are at the ready
While caviar, coffee and assorted entree on queue.
The revelers wearing leis and party hats
Waiting for the stroke of midnight and the New Year.

The bewitching hour was heralded in with a chime
As everyone got into frenzied and passionate embrace
The Serenade Band played Auld Lang Syne,
To some couples locked in that midnight kiss
Pledging renewed comradery, friendship, and fun
For the ensuing year of complete bliss and fortune.

Daybreak ©

The sun slowly ascends o'er the craggy mountain,
As the moon grows dim and the stars became few
The bay comes alive with egrets, gulls, and terns.
Awake from their slumber after a tranquil night,
To frolic and engage in another food fight.

The white-crested waves roll in from the ocean,
The breakers crashing against the cliff,
At times, fading to a faint whisper, then calm;
Witnessing the miraculous symmetry of life,
Such soothing aural experience at dawn.

The lush mountain ranges, lit by the sun
Exotic flora, fauna, sand, sea, and sky
Makes the entire vista something to ponder,
A chance to embrace the serenity of nature,
Enamored by the heavenly beauty and serenity

Alas! Morning has come to the world.
The birds herald the break of dawn,
Small jewels of dew drops are seen
On the frail silky cobwebs
Strewn overnight by tiny spiders.

A of plethora of variegated butterflies
Came floating on the fragrant blossoms.
Out on the shimmering turquoise water
Myriad of lucid crystals from the sun's light
An artistic display by Mother Nature.

Beauties on the Beach ©

Invaded by humans seeking titillation
Children frolic in the sand, sun and swells
Families and friends busy reveling.
The nature lovers gather drift-wood and shells
Gulls overhead diving and dipping
As the beach revelers relish in sand castles.

See the exotic native species so courtly
Always elegant, poised and refined
Known for their unique style and gaiety
Nesting in the sand or under a tree.
They are among God's finest creation
Showing off their bright plumage and beauty.

Bikini-clad figures on the beach
Or under secluded waterfalls
Admire them, but do not touch!
Amiable, modest, and personable
Of unique and distinctive features
Are the lovely Jamaican Beauties.

Sailing on the turquoise waters
To the beat of pulsating reggae rhythms
A catamaran loaded with revelers
Sail fluttering in the tropical breeze
A locale of fun and frolicking
The exhilarating Dunn's River Falls.

Don't Be Crude ©

Hold It! You foul mouthed one!
You are venting vibes of decadence
Those obscenities are like your face.
Please be cognizant of children's presence
Don't be a degradation to the human race.

Your sordid language is confounding,
Incessantly swearing while conversing,
For any anyone within earshot, it is degrading
You parents brought you on this planet.
Let them be proud of your deportment.

Does swearing makes everybody proud,
Prove self-control and super intellect
Or show a fine example of your character,
To make your discourse more pleasant;
Or is it a distinctive sign of your culture?

Is your eloquence pleasing to everyone?
Impress people of your excellent education
Leave no doubt about good breeding;
A respectable role model to children,
Or does it show your level of spirituality?

Open your eyes, your ears and brain,
Engage in discourse and education.
Think, plan, and act with integrity
And inculcate the seeds of ambition.
That you may live a life of dignity.

Corridor of Death ©

There is a bridge, the famous Flat Bridge
Over the infamous Rio Cobre River.
Nestled in the picturesque Bog Walk Gorge
Where the troubled waters meander
Over and under this historic 1770 structure.

This unique historical infrastructure
Enabled passage of millions - business and leisure
To cross over the cool and deadly river
As pedestrians, or on every modern transport
To traverse its platform of stone and mortar.

Invariably, some never get pass the haunted site
As the legendary indentured servants of the past
Seek more souls for their Good Friday noon fiesta
From among the churlish or petulant lead foot
For an eternal baptism with long gone ancestors.

The Bog Walk Tube was another disaster
During June 1904, in this infamous corridor.
Thirty-three hard working artisans were digested
In the defunct hydro-electric turbine station
That supplied electricity to city and it's environed.

Flat Bridge -*The oldest bridge in Jamaica originally constructed as a rudimentary crossing about 1660s with logs,* **piles and braces and again interlaced with masonry** *sometime about 1724 – 1770, when the road through the Bog Walk Gorge was being built. Subsequently, after flood rains washed it away, the current structure was re-built about 1774. It remained flat so that water could pass over and under it - hence its longevity, over 350+ years.*

The Good Life ©

My life is not about luxury or excess,
But for love and peaceful coexistence.
Someone with whom I can reciprocate;
And consummate her marvelous splendor.
With such fervor no words can express.
An exquisite package of rapture.

Feeling her gentle hands over my body,
To relieve my stress, and be consoled.
Buoyed by her erogeneity.
And the yielding cushion of her bosom
Such a marvelous person by my side.
To fill my being with joy and pride

Fully engulfed in her tight embrace
Hoping the moments will never end
Immersed in her charms and grace,
Her warm smile, a touch of her hands,
Momentarily shutting out the world
With the alluring tone of her voice.

I yearn for health and longevity,
The sense of belonging in friendship,
That very modest and special person,
With a love to nurture and build on,
Who is willing to be a lover and a friend
To pledge my unconditional devotion.

I Am a Born Jamaican ©

What makes me strong?	My heritage
What makes me weak?	My fears
What makes me whole?	My God
What keeps me standing?	My faith
What makes me compassionate?	My selflessness
What makes me honest?	My Integrity
What sustains my mind?	My quest for knowledge
What teaches me all lessons?	My mistakes
What lifts my head high?	My pride
What if I can't go on?	Not an option
What makes me victorious?	My courage to climb
What makes me competent?	My confidence
What makes me amiable?	My insatiable essence
What makes me smart?	My intellect
What makes me human?	My heart
Who says I need Love?	I do
What empowers me?	My creativity
Who am I?	A Jamaican Man

The Five T's

Time - Give the precious gift of my attention,
Talk -   Someone to communicate our interests,
Tease - Someone who have a sense of humor,
Trust - Someone whom I can confide in, and
Touch- Shared tactile ecstasy.

Take **PRIDE** in yourself.

Pride
Respect
Integrity
Diligence
Excellence

TEACHING - Moments of Leadership

Time – spend time to discover the real issue
Exposure – find out what others have done
Assistance - have your team study all angles
Creativity – brainstorm multiple solutions
Hit It – implement the best solution

Golden Rules for Living

If you open it, close it.
If you turn it on, turn it off.
If you unlock it, lock it up.
If you break it, admit it.
If you can't fix it, call in someone who can.
If you borrow it, return it.
If you value it, take care of it.
If you make a mess, clean it up.
If you move it, put it back.
If it belongs to someone else and you want to use it, get permission.
If it is none of your business, do not ask questions or eavesdrop.
If it's not broken, do not fix it.
If it will brighten someone's day, say it.
If it will tarnish someone's reputation, keep it to yourself.
If you don't have a cent, and you're polite to everyone, you can get through life.
Waste not, want not.

Adapted Anonymous

Life and Work Management

Whatever one's station is in life, whether low or high status, strive to be the best station-manager ever. It's not the position that is important, it's the disposition of the person manning the station that is most important.   Consider the myriad of people whose lives can be impacted by a simple error.
Success only comes with hard work. Some people may say and do otherwise, but anything else could fail in an instant, although nothing is guaranteed.
Excellent work ethics will always be acknowledged, even when it appears no one is taking notes. A conscientious worker will always be prepared for any opportunity that may arise to move up the career ladder. .
In every organization, someone has to do the 'dirty work', but doing that 'dirty' job in the most proficient way, will progressively pave the way to a cleaner, and more lucrative positions. A splendid work ethics and reputation will put anyone in the draw for the jackpot.
Hitting the jackpot can only happen when preparedness meets opportunity = LUCK.

Ken Damally

Finding a Good Man

It's often said "Good men are hard to Find".
Good men are indeed all around.
Women pass them on the streets, in the malls, at work, or in the parks.
Some women would not recognize a good man, if they don't know what to look for.
A Good man/husband, is merely a good son who is groomed well and mature.
Material assets don't make a good man, affluence is illusionary and fleeting.
A Good Man has rich qualities that embody compassion, honesty, and integrity.
He may not wear a suit, drive an expensive automobile, or have a Manhattan condo.
He's usually not flashy or wealthy enough to turn heads.
He may not be Adonis, but its better he's got your back than turn your head.
A good man doesn't necessarily have to agree with everything you say.
Healthy discourse and sincerity in actions are more important.
His opinions are valid and should not lead to absurd acrimony.
No one is perfect, so a good man may not meet all your criteria.
He is human with frailties mixed in with his wonderful strength.
He needs your love, respect, support, trust, and understanding.
A good man isn't insecure about his wife having greater achievements.
He is her number one confidant and motivator, and shoulders to cry on.
A good woman will bring her good man along with her as she excels.

The size or value of his *"presents"* are not as important as his *"presence"*.
Don't judge a good man by Hollywood or TV's standards – that's fairytale.
To say there are no good men is not totally true – parents can produce them.
Abundant fruits begin with healthy roots, nurture and tender the orchard well. ~K Damally

R-E-S-P-E-C-T

We are all human beings, and we are all equal too.
Treat others the way you want them to treat you.
Respect is paramount in any entity – bedroom, boardroom, national, or international.
It is the oil that that reduces friction and conflicts almost every time.
Mutual respect facilitates better communication, enhance relationships and a magnificent morale booster. Sadly, some millennials have drifted into the dismal abyss of anarchy, bigotry, and misogyny No civilization ever collapse because people were too respectful of each other.

Ladies Decorum 101 –
A Poignant Message

Two young ladies arrived a Meeting wearing clothes that were quite revealing their body parts. Here is what the Chairman told them.   He took a good look at them and made them sit. Then he said something that, they might never forget in their life.   He looked at them straight in the eyes and said; "ladies, everything that God made valuable in this world is well covered and hardly to see, find or get.

1. Where do you find diamonds?   Deep down in the ground, covered and protected.

2. Where do you find pearls?   Deep down at the bottom of the ocean, covered up and protected in a beautiful shell.

3. Where do you find gold?   Way down in the mine, covered over with layers of rock and to get them, you have to work hard & dig deep down to get them.
He looked at them with serious eyes and said;
"Your body is sacred & unique" You are far more precious than gold, diamonds and pearls, and you should be covered too:
"So he added that, if you keep your treasured mineral just like gold, diamond and pearls, deeply covered up, a reputable mining organization with the requisite machinery will fly down and conduct years of extensive exploration.

First, they will contact your government (family), sign professional contracts (wedding) and mine you professionally (legal marriage).But if you leave your precious minerals uncovered on the surface of the earth, you always attract a lot of illegal miners to come and mine you illegally. Everybody will just pick up their crude instruments and just have a dig on you just freely like that. Keep your bodies deeply covered so that it invites only professional miners to chase you.

****

We need to teach our young women to distinguish between:

A man who flatters her, and a man who compliments her.

A man who spends money on her and a man who invests in her.

A man who views her as property and a man who views her properly

A man who lusts after her and man who loves her.

A man who believes he's a gift to women and a man who believes she's a gift to him.

And then, most importantly, we need to groom, and teach our young men to be that kind of man.

Let us all encourage our wives, friends and daughters to dress well and decent!   *Illuzone - www.illuzone.net*

<u>Trust is earned not won</u>
<u>and respect should be mutual.</u>

What makes a man in my eyes is the show of respect, trust, loyalty to relationships (regarding all aspects of a relationship, i.e., not talking out of the relationship to others), kindness, tenderness, compassion, understanding and someone who always tries to see and believe the best of one first. Basically, a man who isn't more interested in keeping up an image but one who is humble.

A man who shows respect and good manners to all at all times, will win the heart of a woman he loves and this woman will want to respect him, and if he continues showing her respect and good manners, he will never lose her respect and trust but this goes to say about anyone's trust and respect as unfortunately many times people show respect and trust until they think they possess/own the other and the respect and good manners go out the window and then obviously respect and trust is destroyed. Show respect and trust, and you will receive respect and trust as it is earned.

Stéphanie Carter

Reference Guide to Friends' Personality Styles

There are four personality styles that are generally applicable acquaintances. These are experiential observations, and should not be construed as scientific analytical data. Again, no two individuals are alike.

Analyzers:

Analyzers are usually orderly, procedural, precise, quiet, conservative, and does not crave accolades.
Efficient, conventional, and prefers organized personal surroundings.
Attire is seldom colorful or trendy, and likes conservative grey.
Speak quietly and carefully using choice of words for precision and effect.
Slow to make decisions due to need for data and research.
More serious and thoughtful, sometimes can be misconstrued as being aloof.
When approaching, minimize small talk, present adequate data, research, and provide substantive supporting exhibits – facts not fiction.
Follow up with exchange of written information.

Controller:

Usually result oriented, impatient, high energy, and very time conscious.
Tend to prefer dark furniture and fixtures, symbols, pictures, gadgets and symbols to emphasize ego.
Dark or high contrast colors, jewelry and accessories.

Demonstrate firm handshake, aggressive body language, loud and rapid speech to get a point across. Quicker to judge and make rash decisions.

Likes to tell, rather than be told, intense eye contact.

Of course, likes to control, must be their way to make a decision, or the highway.

They are serious, does not share feelings or expression of emotion.

When approaching, be assertive, but avoid confrontation - they are averse to small talk.

Make appointments and be prompt, but expect tardiness on their part.

Give options and close quickly and make strong follow up.

Promoter:

They are outgoing, crave center of attention, motivating, result oriented and enthused.

They tend to like warm to bright décor, accessories, pictures of people, trophies, posters of motivational articles, and business statistics.

Their attire tends to be flamboyant, colorful, and likes trendy styles of accessories.

They exhibit a wide range of hand gestures, inflections, jokes and stories - humorous.

Typically, poor time management, may digress from a task, procrastinate, or fail to follow up. Prefers talking to listening, very spontaneous, high-risk taker, talk and shares feelings.

The approach to a promoter should be personable, as they like compatibility and tend to lash out if pressured or abruptly end the discourse. They listen well, like to keep on track, emphasize results, and use dynamic language to facilitate information transfer.

Supporter:

Supporters are warm, open, team player, caring, supportive, and a good listener.
They maintain inviting home and surroundings, pictures of people and scenic places.
Attire usually reflect mood and can be warm to bright colors, a few grays.
Behavioral attitude involves a soft voice, warm and friendly eye contact, occasionally introverted, carefully worded speech, and a relaxed posture.
They prefer to analyze the project before making a decision, get the input and approval of the impacted parties to make sure all hands are on deck.
When approaching a supporter, pertinent small talk to get them talking is permissible, especially when soliciting their help.   Offer assurances to allay any doubt, or they may acquiesce half-heartedly.

ANONYMOUS

****

Human Relations − Acrostics

Have self-control.
Understand others' viewpoint.
Make others' interests your own.
Admit it when you're wrong.
Never make promises you can't keep

Reason: don't argue.
Explain thoroughly.
Lead: don't drive
Avoid snap judgments.
Take care of little things
Inform people of changes affecting them.
Observe and listen
Never criticize in public.
Stress the positive.   -

Hotel Sales Management Association

Instructions for Life

The Dalai Lama

1. Recognize that great love and achievements involve great risk.
2. When you lose, don't lose the lesson.
3. Follow the three R's:
    Respect for self
    Respect for others and
    Responsibility for all your actions.
4. Remember that not getting what you want could be a wonderful stroke of luck.
5. Learn the rules so you know how to break them properly.
6. Don't let a little dispute injure a great friendship.
7. When you realize you've made a mistake, take steps to correct it immediately.
8. Spend some time alone every day.
9. Open your arms to change, but don't let go of your values.
10. Remember that silence is sometimes the best answer.
11. Live a good honorable life, so you can enjoy it a second time when you're old.
12. A loving atmosphere in your home is the foundation for your life.
13. In disagreements deal only with the current situation. Don't bring up the past.
14. Share your knowledge. It's a way to achieve immortality.
15. Be gentle with the earth.
16. Once a year, go someplace you've never been before.
17. Remember that the best relationship is where love exceeds need for each other.
18. Judge your success by what you had to give up in order to get it.
19. Approach love and cooking with reckless abandon.
20. Remember to say "I Love You" to your loved ones – and really mean it!

The Ideals of a Loving Relationship

What are the obstacles that keep us from loving?
We can find many of them hidden in the Apostle Paul's classic treatise on love.
Here we can find both the qualities of love and its obstacles that hinder healthy relationships:

Love is patient.   The Obstacle — Impatience

Impatience describes a person whose own agenda is more important than that of anyone else.   It's my way or the highway is their mantra.
Typically, they lose their cool for no good reason other than not having their own way.
These outbursts come as a surprise to the persons on the receiving end who do not see it coming.   This person has little time or care for others' concerns.
An impatient person must constantly be entertained and quickly loses interest in people if they are not filling a need in his or her own life.
The Greek word Paul uses for "patience" describes a person who has been wronged and has the power to avenge himself, but chooses not to.
Impatience seeks revenge.   Patience does not.

Love is kind.   The Obstacle — Unkindness

Some people think kindness is synonymous with weakness. Therefore, they reason, one cannot obtain strength and power through kindness.
Those who constantly see themselves in competition with others tend to be unkind.
A latent sense of inferiority is another cause for unkindness. In contrast, love is the readiness to enhance the life of another person.

Love is trusting.   The Obstacle — Jealousy

Love naturally means concern.   As love grows, concern for the beloved also grows.
But quite often, without one realizing it, this concern can become possessive. Jealousy entails total possession—it must have exclusive rights to another person even their thoughts and desires.
Where there's love, there's jealousy, but it must be tempered with respect for the person - not smothering.
Living and working with such people is oppressive and amounts to emotional abuse.
This emotion has the power to overwhelm and destroy the most sound and secure relationship, and the most rational person.

Love is humble.   The Obstacle — Arrogance

Various Bible translations use different words to describe this obstacle to love:
Boastful, crass, proud, eager to impress, braggart, exalted ego, and seek excessive validation for accolades - "How great thou art.
They avoid sharing their affection or emotion, and does not show compassion unconditionally, or participate in any meaningful discourse.
Aggressive body language and loudness is a common trait. "Don't tell me what to do!!!"
Their real purpose is to put others down while trying to elevate themselves. "The know-it all".
 Charity, Hope and Love - The greatest of these is love.
*** Unknown***

Philosophy of Life by Ken Damally

◎ Good looks catch the eye, and may be desirable, but a good personality that embodies honesty, intellect, integrity and modesty, are the most essential traits that catches the heart.
Real attraction comes from within – Compassion, Intelligence, Resilience, and Strength.

◎ Women have bodies designed to sustain life, but they should define their own world, be admired for their abilities, brains, and competence - not just their bodies.
Their best revenge for implicit gender bias or misogyny is to be a success.

◎ Affluence enamors many friends, hearty laughter and good connections, but the down-trodden and destitute is forsaken, left to cry, groan, and moan alone.

◎ It's more prudent to choose conference and cooperation, above conflict or confrontation.
Engage in productive dialogue with civility, decency, and trust.
Always be empathetic and open, in trying to resolve problems.

◎ Luck is that moment when preparedness meets opportunity.
Stay ready so you do not have to get ready.

◎ No civilization ever collapses because people were too civil or respectful of each other.

◎ We have lost the true value of civil and honest discourse, which would help us recognize our commonality. Hypocrisy, inconsistency, vitriol and vulgarity have perverted our society and laid fertile ground for the worst among us to engage in anarchy and extremism – both in politics and religion.

✺ Adversity is a powerful process for shifting our attention and energy towards good things that we were inattentive to before. Be grateful, smile that it happened to open our eyes and recognize the lapse in our judgment, then strive towards a more positive developmental path that produce benefits to our lives.

✺ Any condition that is conducive to the development of organisms, will definitely enable their emergence. An example of this is the flawed legislations with loopholes, or discriminatory edicts. They will certainly be breached and exploited by people with nefarious intent, because they also lay the fertile ground for anarchy and criminality.

✺ Experience comes from making bad judgments;
Our ambitious human nature usually tempts us to make ill-advised choices.
Talent evolves from constant practice, which in turn leads to progress.   Good judgment then evolves out of experience.

✺ A person who never made a mistake, never attempted anything new.   Sometimes you may succeed, you learn, or discover a breakthrough, but it's human to err, that's why erasers were created.

✺ The longest journey begins with the first step.
The secret of achieving goals is getting started.

✺ We tend to be overly cautious due to fear, and that can make us timid.   A relationship without trust, is like a car without petrol, you can stay in it all you want, but it will not go anywhere. Waiting, wishing, and worrying are the greatest time-wasters.

◎ You never know a churlish person until that person demonstrate, orate, or write something absurd. A hot-tempered person stirs up conflict, but the one who is patient calms a quarrel

◎ Intelligence is like a river, the deeper it is, the softer it flows. It is the soft dewdrops or rain that sustain the flora, not the boom of the thunder.
Parallel to this - Empty barrel makes the most noise, or the narrowest minds vent the loudest.

◎ One fool makes many, so never disregard the power of a group of ignorant, insensate people who have been effectively brainwashed by propaganda media with false narratives. Considering the exponential effect of the many suckers born every minute, their actions could create ominous consequences for society. Misinformation always attract people of low morality.

◎ Hatred, ethnic bias, and intolerance of others emanate from acquired internal mechanisms – according to how we perceive ourselves. If we truly love ourselves, then we would love others unconditionally. It is the adverse intra-personal view that people propagate – which is at the root of all the troubles paralyzing this otherwise wonderful world we live in.

◎ Possibilities are endless, but for most of us, they remain undiscovered. Instead of conceptualizing, we sit on our archaic ideas and mores, clinging to the things that are whimsical and vain – being overly cautious.
We conform to the familiar, the comfortable, and the mundane. For the most part, our lives are mediocre instead of exciting, fulfilling and thrilling.
We should be daring - destroy that branch of fear we cling to, develop the courage to free ourselves to the glory of flight into new adventures and horizons.

☀ Our society suffers from the perennial over-abundance of obscene arrogance, cockiness, flawed, misleading, and false arguments which are everywhere, and spiraling the country to an exponentially descending low. Some of the insensitivity emanated from 'idolized' politicians and charlatans, whose only objective is to obfuscate their arrogant and ignorant followers, some of whom are morally inferior, suffering from low emotional or social intelligence – otherwise called 'racists or racism, by way of effective brainwashing. Misinformation always attracts people of low morality.
Perhaps, if the people would use logic as a medium of intellectual self-defense and quality control, they could insulate themselves from these bombardments, and be better able to make critical decisions.

☀ Bigotry, misogyny, or racism is an acquired psychotic affliction found in people who feels morally inferior, suffering from a low emotional state of being, or lacking social intelligence. The practice is spread by way of effective propaganda media. A racist in uniform, robe, or a suit will never admit to their derisive assertions, which comes from within.
Unfortunately, we still have vestiges of anarchy, bigotry, misogyny, and racism - universally.

☀ A creative mind is like a parachute; it only works when it is open
Once it opens up to new experiences, it never reverts to its former state.
It provides the framework for common-sense logic, and problem-solving prowess.
It is not a vessel to be filled, but is a fire to be constantly stoked for a brighter future.

☼ Beware of those actions, and faith of despots that is based on their own ideas, feelings, and what they think is right – rather than what is ethically and morally right. Restricting assembly, free speech, and the press is the introductory tool used by despots and dictators. They utilize their own propaganda media to obfuscate the populace in order to divide and conquer. We now have a new façade adopted from established dictatorships called: "Alternative Facts" or "Fake Facts", which can also be called "Effective Propaganda". Effective propaganda media is <u>NOT about Facts and Policy</u>, it IS about emotions, and used to energize people who feels morally inferior, and are of low social intelligence. A foolish faith in a despot's authority may be the worst enemy of truth.

☼ Kind deeds, truth and sincerity will stand the rigors of time, and replicate into eternity. They are always the strongest arguments – beautiful, immortal and perpetual,
Strive for, and have a relentless expectation for excellence in honesty, ethics, and integrity
We should all embrace the love of family, friends, and extend good will to all.
.

☼ Some people find it much easier and deft to criticize everyone and everything,
But find it very difficult to create, encourage, praise, or think and suggest a solution to a situation, or to advance the discourse.

☼ Intellectual growth should commence at birth and cease only at death. *Albert Einstein*

☼ It's no disgrace to be born in the ghetto or gutter.
But it's absolutely disgraceful having the desire to stay there.

◉ Arrogance, ignorance, and lack of common-sense are the deadliest impediment to any civilize discourse that could facilitate a more cohesive society. Intelligence is a necessary tool for civility, and to respect the other person's opinion without becoming enraged or obscene. Our most urgent task in our time is to build a global society where people of all color and persuasions can live together in peace and harmony. We are tolerant toward others when we tolerate ourselves.

◉ It has become appallingly obvious that the era of social media technology has fostered a great deal of anti-social behavior that exceeded our humanity. Automated propaganda media which disseminate falsehoods, vitriol, and poison intelligent discourse, are a real threat to civil society.

◉ "We are going mentally soggy through the culture of TV, which fosters very passive mentalities as well as shortened attention span. (People are reading less about civic or current affairs.)
If civilization can be said to be built on trains of thought, then we have a situation in which the TV, a bumper car of emotions - has replaced the train of thought."   *James H. Billington*

◉ We were endowed with two ears, and oftentimes we may hear, but do not listen, or comprehend important messages that could impact our lives.

◉ It is the things we **'know'** that are no longer **'so'**, that blind us to opportunities.   We fail to realize our incredible potential as humans - because of fear.

◉ The internet was intended to educate, entertain, enlighten, and integrate people of the world into one global community – not to obfuscate. Ironically, some people use it anonymously to open up a toxic dungeon of anarchy, character assassinations, hate, intolerance, misinformation, a toxic mix of lies, innuendo, obscenities, xenophobia, and resentment, and other invidious epithets, that they would not dare utter in a face-to-face discourse. Our most urgent task in our time, is to build a global society where people of all ethnicity and persuasions can live together in peace and harmony. We are tolerant toward others when we tolerate ourselves.

◉ A good man is merely a good son well-groomed and grown up. Children live what they experience or learn from adults.
Teach the children about qualities that embody compassion, honesty, integrity, Respect for self, and humanity, to transform our surly society. When the apple falls from the tree, the tree loses its responsibility.

◉ A dissembler (hypocrite) can only see the faults of others as being glaring and repulsive, but fail to recognize their own faults or stupidity. This is synonymous with a driver who is oblivious that their own headlights on high beam are blinding other drivers, but sees others high beam as reprehensible.

◉ Great leaders did not set out to be leaders, they set out to make a difference in the world. They earn respect as leaders of character, empathy, ethics, integrity and influence.
A great leader never usurps their rank or position. Their focus is always be about the goal.
True Leadership is about achieving the optimal result possible - a job done well.

◉ Respect is stopping to think how one's actions affect others – simply good manners.
Be considerate of others feelings in deciding what to do, or say, that could be offensive.

☉ We also have two eyes to observe and gain knowledge - but fail see the beautiful world with all that nature provides around us, and then we have only one mouth with a tongue to orate words of wisdom. We should therefore endeavor to use our God given attributes accordingly.

☉ We should all be kind and respectful in our attitudes and interactions with each other. No number of apologies can retract defamatory, derogatory or obscene utterances.
Our attitude can literally determine our altitude.

☉ Academic achievements and wealth do not measure intelligence, or leadership ability.
Prospective leaders must engage their pedantry in tandem with common-sense, civility, ethics and integrity, then that mélange will create a more rounded intelligent person capable of leading others.
Courage is doing what you are afraid to do, the power to let go of the familiar and mundane, and explore new territory - to fulfill your destiny.

☉ As the dawn precedes the day, so is the child that grows up to be an adult.
The fact that many parents, teachers, evangelicals, politicians and civil-rights organizations engage in hypocrisy, inconsistency, and tolerate and make excuses for the despicable and destructive behavior of so many young people, is a gross betrayal of the memory, struggle, sacrifice, sweat and blood of our ancestors. No civilization ever collapses because people were too civil or respectful of each other.

☉ No matter how educated, talented, wealthy, or how suave anyone thinks they are, it's the way how they treat people ultimately tells how much character they possess.
Character embodies compassion, ethics, and integrity, which is paramount for success.

⚙ There can be no greater feeling than knowing you've achieved your goals.   Success only comes with the individual's hard work.   No one can take away your education and honor - you must give it away yourself.

⚙ Ability is what you're capable of doing, and is unique to you.
Motivation determines what you do - to validate your worth.
Attitude determines how well you do it.
Ambition is wanting to succeed against all odds to achieve desired goals.

⚙ Any person can be what they want to be; it's all up to the individual. Socio-economic barriers are external obstacles to desired goals; but aspirations, motivation and values are internal mechanism that can propel one to success.

⚙ The ability to learn and be successful is dynamic, and is not a sprint, if the mind is strong, desired goals can be met.
It is a marathon that entails perseverance and true grit.

⚙ If a person is of strong mind and **determined** to learn and help them self, no one can stop them, but if that person is **NOT** willing to learn and work, no one can help them.

⚙ It's **NOT** one's *position* that makes them happy or unhappy, it's their *disposition*.
If you are happy and healthy, then you have more than any millionaire does.

⚙ Dress to impress, be authentic to attract positive vibes, and to encourage respect.
Know your self-value and self-worth, and don't dress and behave like a suspect.

☼ Count your blessings every day and do not let disappointments get you down. Not everyone can be famous, but they can be great in service.
Rise, take note, re-evaluate your status quo, and strive for more positive goals.

☼ Don't spend time beating on a wall, hoping to transform it into a door.
You are wasting your time if you are not achieving positive results from engaging in any activity, experience, or a relationship.

☼ The mind is like a parachute; it only works when it is open. It is not a vessel to be filled, but is a fire to be constantly stoked

☼ The lips of the wise spread knowledge, but the mouth of fools obfuscate.
Wise men do not need the advice, but fools will not heed it

☼ We oftentimes engage a misnomer when we use the term Rich to describe someone's affluence – their material assets.
A **RICH** person is a well-rounded individual with enduring high standard of ethics in all aspects of humanity – compassion, gratitude, honesty and kindness. They can attract and sustain genuine friendships and rise above the trappings of opulence.
WEALTH - is materialism which is fleeting; it can make some individuals apathetic.
It is better to strive for good health and purity – it is more beneficial for enjoying any wealth.

☼ The orated or written word is like a stone that is thrown Once released to any audience, it can never be withdrawn. No number of apologies can negate invidious remarks, or misinformation.

☼ A simple smile and hello is the shortest distance between two people, just like your candle which loses nothing when it lights another. Respect for life and humanity could lead to many opportunities. A growl or a dour countenance can lose you valued acquaintances.
Kind words, or humor will get people to smile, and become your friends.

☼ Great ideas can evolve from the most ordinary event, or person, if the other person has the vision to comprehend it. A wise person can learn from a fool, but conversely, it's almost impossible.

☼ Revenge can create a repercussion greater than the hurt itself. The way out of trouble is never as easy, and as simple as the way in.

☼ "A mind that is stretched by a new experience can never go back to its old dimensions".   *Oliver Wendell Holmes*

☼ Good temper, like a sunny day, sheds a brightness over everything, it is the sweetener of toil and the soother of disquietude.   *Washington Irving*

☼ "It is better to tell the truth than to lie, better to be free than a slave, better to have knowledge than be ignorant."
– *H.L. Mencken*

☼ Ideally, we should all be able to think for ourselves, and use our **"Power of logic", to** do what is ethically and morally acceptable to chart our own destiny.
Logic teaches us to value the truth, to understand that life is a source of experience to live with love, and all the richness life has to offer.
Life is not measured by the breaths we take, but by the moments that take our breath away.

☼ A creative mind is like a parachute; it only works when it is open, and provide the framework for common-sense logic, and problem-solving prowess.
It enables one to realize the power of observing things in an entirely different way.

☼ Integrity is ethical behavior, and being trustworthy always, even when no one is looking.
Do the right thing and it will gratify some people and astonish the skeptics.
Always maintain the character of an honest person. One is only as good as their private standard.

☼ Hope and expectation are the belief that something desired is going to materialize.
Don't try too hard, the best things come when you least expect them to.

☼ Disappointment evolves out of expectations – real or unreal.
Do not blame others for disappointing you,
Blame yourself for expecting too much from them.

☼ Perception is the process by which we come to understand ourselves and others. We cannot always absorb everything we hear and see; therefore, we must be selective.
However, differences in perception have a direct correlation to our senses as we tend to engage the analytical filter to disregard those things countering our expectations or wishes.

☼ Diplomacy is telling someone to digress to hell in such plausible manner that the person eagerly anticipates the trip.

☼ Perspective can undoubtedly influence perception. Everybody views the world differently - like the perspective of a giraffe vs a turtle.   Too often semantics hinder communication - rather than stimulate it, when seemingly opposing points of view can both be mistaken.

☼ "Your candle loses nothing when you use it to light another, It will certainly make the world much brighter place for its people. Use your candle to enlighten rather than curse the darkness of the universe."   *Eleanor Roosevelt*

☼ Embrace challenges no matter how daunting they may seem; they make you stronger.
Strive for, and have a relentless expectation for excellence in honesty, ethics, and integrity.

☼ If you constantly associate with negative people, you will not likely to have a positive outlook on life. A wise person can learn from a fool, but conversely, it's almost impossible.

☼ Not achieving one's goal is conciliatory – having NO goals to achieve is deplorable.
Be consistent with practice, gain experience, then perfection and success are attainable.
Success is most often achieved by those who never lose courage or curiosity.

☼ By consciously directing your thoughts in a positive direction, you can change your life and perspectives to achieve ultimate satisfaction. The past is a place of reference not a place of permanent residence.

☼ Do not do, or say anything out of desperation; it could adversely affect judgment, and also could be a turnoff to others.

◎ Diplomacy, dialogue and détente are the most prudent alternative to hostility.
We must live together as intelligent human beings or perish together as fools.

◎ Conferences or discussions are more prudent than arguments. An argument usually is to determine WHO is right, but a discussion is to ascertain WHAT happen, and HOW it happens; but most exceptional is WHY it happens, and then work towards making it better.
Engage in productive ideas to enhance the discourse for alternative solutions.

◎ Extraordinary and unique experiences give life to everlasting memories.
We have two ears, two eyes and one mouth – we should use them accordingly.

◎ "Some people's idea of free speech is that they are free to say what they like, but if anyone retorts - it's an outrage".
Winston Churchill

◎ We derive the heart of our culture, the foundation of our state laws, and the shared morality of daily life from some parts of The Bible. If human were angels, we would not need government, or the security forces. We are only as good as our private standard.
Without laws, wise men would live the same – showing love and respect for each other.

◎ The person who challenges or responds to an indirect inference, is undoubtedly the culpable one whose conscience was triggered by guilt.
(In Jamaican parlance: "throw me corn, but I no call no fowl".)

❂ Any representative - ecumenical or political, should be authentic, ethical, ardently render service, or administer to the affairs of those being represented, without personal aggrandizement. Anyone devoid of these qualities lack professionalism and is corrupt.

❂ A bigot, a kleptomaniac, a rapist, or schizophrenic will never, ever concede to their afflictions.

❂ "Never go to war where there are no spoils. Choose your battles wisely and make sure that what you fight for is worth the price you pay.
War does not determine who is right, it only determines those who are left."

❂ If you think you are too minuscule, or not important enough to make a difference, then try ignoring a fire ant in your undergarment.
The power of one person can exponentially change the world to make it a better place.

❂ Some people invoke their constitutional rights conveniently when they act despicably, or make disparaging comments about another person. They totally ignore the other person's constitutional rights of liberty, peaceful coexistence, and freedom of speech, respect, or their right for a rebuttal. -

❂ Mankind is always seeking adventure, or for a meaning to their lives. Some people search for life-escapes in alcohol, drugs, materialism, or other perverted pursuits. Unfortunately, in their fervent quest, they oftentimes lapse into a state of decadence or demise. They digest myriad of oral feculence from any charlatan that comes along; be it religious, political, or a village lawyer - without using logic to evaluate the verbiage for themselves, in order to make more prudent decisions about their own lives.

☼ The biggest prize for politicians is the people who are NOT well informed and cannot use logic as quality control to make prudent decisions for themselves. If the political charlatans and hypocrites can obfuscate enough of their ignorant constituents to garner their votes, then they cash in big, and do as they please - without any accountability.

☼ Cultivating intellect or logic takes hard work, similar to the effort it takes ascending a hill. Conversely, it takes very little effort to descend into the valley of apathy, arrogance, ignorance, misogyny, and misinformation. Intellectual growth should commence at birth and cease only at death.

☼ You may never be an interesting person, or a success with gossipers if you mind you own business - Hear no evil, see no evil, and speak no evil.
Don't talk about yourself; it'll be done when you leave.

☼ A true friend is someone who reaches for your hand and touches your heart. Don't waste your time with anyone who isn't willing to reciprocate friendship.

☼ Kindness and gratitude is the oil that takes friction out of life.
The heart that loves is always young and can help spread peace with ease. Tolerance, love, and trust are the keys to success.

☼ Do not feel bad about growing old, it's a privilege denied to many. From aging comes wisdom, influence, innovation, that spurs longevity.

☼ Love is a thing that is never out of season;
Let's keep the lamps of friendship burning with the oil of love. The sun sets in the west, but friendship rises in the heart and sets after death.

☀ No one is an island; don't be isolated –
Build bridges to make acquaintances and span the void.

☀ Don't be is such a hurry to condemn a person because he doesn't do what you do, or think as you think.   There was a time when you didn't know what you know today.

☀ It is a nice feeling to know someone loves you, misses you, and needs you. However, it feels much better to know
that once someone comes into your life
They will never be forgotten and will reciprocate the mutual friendship.

☀ In Life, you realize that there is a purpose for everyone you meet.
Some will test you; some will use you, and some will teach you.
But the most important ones, are those who bring out the best in you,
Show gratitude, respect, and acceptance for who you are.
They are the friends always worth keeping around.

☀ "Children and teenagers need adult guidance, parental nurturing, love, support, and their **Presence.**
They don't need criticism, dereliction, judgement, or a plethora of **Presents**."

☀ "It is easier to build strong and educated children, than to repair broken men or women"   *Frederick Douglas*

☀ "When professionalism is lacking, there is a slow drift downwards toward mediocrity.
Dossiers become full of trite and lifeless information, and incapable of opening up lofty perspectives," **Pope Francis**

☼ We are constantly bombarded with false, flawed, and misleading information everywhere.
From merchants competing for your money, politicians vying for votes, or others hoping to fill their coffers. Our best self-defense is to engage logic – analyze the facts, think, plan, and engage sound reasoning as quality control tools in order to validate the pedantry, and shape our own moral views.

☼ Forests grow from seedlings, and when those seedlings are nurtured properly, and mature, they become magnificent foliage. Parents should teach children to be that person they would desire for themselves, - as a life-partner. As the dawn precedes the day, so is the child that is taught well, and grows up to be a productive and respectable citizen.

☼ When we train our youth to take responsibility in the development of themselves and their community, they become valuable assets to society.   Parents who teach their children good work habits, is better than giving them a fortune. Education and integrity are the key to success.   Ethics and respect for the individual provide an ideal framework for living the good life.   It's good for our family, friends, ourselves, and the universe.

☼ If you think you are too small to make a difference…
Try sleeping with a mosquito in the room.   **Dalai Lama**

☼ A wise man can learn from a fool, but conversely the fool will decry the words of wisdom.

☼ Prudence is virtuous, so be assertive but respectful.
Avoid virulent words that could be averse to your status or decorum.   Engage the brain and apply your ears and eyes to words of knowledge.

✺ Gratitude is a powerful process for shifting your emotions and energy, and channeling it to produce the desired physical benefits to your life.
You never know when kindness and respect will come full circle.

✺ Good thoughts precede Great deeds which translate into ultimate success.
Your action or deed is the script for your reputation.

✺ By consciously directing your thoughts in a positive direction, you can change your life and perspectives to achieve ultimate fulfillment.
The fomentation of anarchy and nefarious vandalism are based on arrogance and ignorance by a few societal malcontents who piggy-back on legitimate causes, with the intent to destabilize society, and tarnish the reputation of the good people in our heterogeneous global community.

✺ Be passionate about meeting challenges, solving problems, and doing a job well to fulfill your destiny. Do not go to work to do a job. Develop a passion for your chosen occupation.

✺ Work can create positive changes in someone's life – one person at a time.

✺ Success is the ultimate result of ambition, full honest effort, and hard work. Even the most successful appreciate accolades, but don't be a glutton for praises.
Fortify yourself with contentment, and don't be averse to constructive criticisms.

✺ Be careful how you treat the people you meet ascending the ladder of success, because your attitude will determine your altitude.
Your descent may be so fast that you become just a blur to those below.

◎ The achievements of great men did not materialize overnight. They muster the courage to do what others were afraid to do. While others party, slept, and procrastinate, they persevere all throughout their plight.

◎ Surround yourself with happy and positive people. Capture their infectious enthusiasm and passion, and they will leave an indelible mark on you, and keep you optimistic.

◎ The stream of life is full with Love and Goodness - just waiting to be embraced; unfortunately, some insidious people make it murky and treacherous for others.

◎ Those who believe the world is a just place, have more optimistic trust in others.
The downside is that they are more vulnerable to those that have nefarious motives.

◎ Happiness is a byproduct of positive attitude, empathy, generosity, and respect which undoubtedly can influence the level of bliss. Think, plan, and act on things that are beautiful, meaningful, productive, and progressively engaged towards life's goals.

◎ "Happiness is when what you think, what you say, and what you do are in harmony."   *Mahatma Gandhi*

◎ Emancipate yourselves from mental slavery: none but ourselves can free our mind.   *Marcus Garvey*

◎ Work is love made visible, exercise your mind, talent and skills for economic prosperity. of course, work is work; that's why it's not called play.
Only in the dictionary success precedes work.

- Watch the pennies and the dollars will take care of themselves.

- No matter what job you have in life, your academic credentials will account for only 5% of your success. Your professional experiences accounts for 15%, and your interpersonal communication skills and passion for the job is 80%.

- "Many people with excellent brains achieve nothing while men with moderate brains can be highly successful if they have the drive to achieve."   *Sir Arthur Lewis*

- When we give someone our time, we actually give a portion of our life that we can never take back.   Our time is our life; and the best present you can give your family and friends.

- Make yourself a better person and recognize yourself,
Before you try to know someone else and expect them to know you.

- Maybe it was ordained for us to meet a few wrong people before meeting the right one.
When we finally meet that person, we can truly be appreciative and grateful.

- Keep a sense of humor, because anger will destroy you.
Act like a child appropriately - if you want to be a happy adult.

- A person with clear conscience is like a badge of courage,
They will have no fear of accusations or doubts,
Because their good deeds evolve from God's presence in them.

◎ "The first of qualities for a great statesman is to be honest. I have, and must have, confidence in the possible virtue of human nature.
To believe all men are honest would-be folly. To not so, is something worse." *John Quincey Adams*

◎ When people hate you, they give you a wicker basket to convey water. *(A Jamaican proverb)*.

◎ "Honesty is one part of eloquence. We persuade others by being in earnest ourselves." *William Hazlitt*

◎ Wealthy people vote their self-interest in every single election.
Why don't the less affluent who suffer most do likewise for the issues that affect them?
ALL ELECTIONS are local - mid-terms are even more important

◎ Perhaps if we train our youth about respect and responsibility, the penal institutions would be short of long-term occupants. Teach our children to become valuable citizens in their communities, and society, then, we may not have to worry about them falling victims to police brutality.

◎ "Stay away from lazy parasites who perch on you to satisfy their needs. They do not come to alleviate your burden; hence their mission is to distract, detract, and extract – to make you live in abject poverty".   Michael Bassey Johnson.

◎ Education does not mean teaching people what they don't know. The resposibility of educators is to teach youth to have respect for those who differ from the customary ways as well as those who conform. Everyone have a profound obligation both to education and to society – to support and strengthen the right to be different, and to create a sound respect for intellectual superiority. - Robert C. Pooley

☼ "Every creature, including the fauna and flora on earth, have shown the amazing ability to respond to music. Therefore, it is my humble tenet that anyone who is not stirred, or responsive to the beautiful sounds of music, is lacking empathy and exhibit attributes of a despot. Simply put:
[A PERSON THAT EMBODIES NO MUSIC WITHIN, BE CAUTIOUS OF SUCH A PERSON]"

☼ The eyes of other people are the eyes that ruin us.
We crave fine clothes, houses, furniture, body contour, skin tone, and jewelry
to satisfy their inquisitive eyes.

KAKISTOCRACY –
Government by the worst persons; a form of government in which the worst persons are in power.

"In order to achieve accountability and efficiency in governance, the electorate should be willing to cross political party-lines to elect the best candidates to represent them. Candidates who have proven, excellent track records in business or politics.
Reject those moronic charlatans backed by "big money", and spew campaign misinformation.
It is the same principle applies when selecting a qualified person for a job in the Private Sector."

☼ Leave the world a bit better whether by
A healthy child, a garden patch, or a
Redeemed social condition;
Play and laugh with enthusiasm
Sing with exultation, to know
That even one life has breathed easier because you've lived.
This is to have succeeded.
Ralph Waldo Emerson (1803-1882)

Bungling Bureaucracy

This is a life-experience story that is common-place in government and the public sector.
"Too many cooks spoil the Broth".

Everyday a conscientious worker Mr. Ant would arrive early for work and started working immediately. He was very proficient in his craft so he did not need an assistant.
He developed and streamlined his production method for making widgets and as he could work without supervision. The widget department was a major profit center for the company. His superiors were delighted that he did not even need to work overtime.
Mr. Ant proficiently met his production goals, and could provide a comfortable lifestyle for his family and himself. This motivated him to work even harder, and he was happy.

One day the CEO, Mr. Lion paid a visit to the department and saw how efficient and organized the department was. He was surprised that Mr. Ant was achieving all this without supervision. Mr. Lion's theorized that if Mr. Ant can work so well without supervision, then he could produce more if he was supervised. He did not consult with Mr. Ant to learn about his proficiency, and perhaps duplicate his method to other departments.

Mr. Lion recruited Supervisor Roach who had extensive supervisory experience and could produce excellent production reports.
Mr. Roach's first decision was to set up a production reports and records archiving system.
He also needed an administrative assistant to help him type his various reports and input for the archiving system.
Since the administrative assistant would be busy most of the time, she needed someone to do archiving of records and monitor phone calls.

Mr. Lion was delighted with Mr. Roach's reports, but wanted him to produce graphs to describe production rates, analyze trends for presentation at his board meetings.
In order to produce the graphs Mr. Roach had to procure a computer and a laser printer.

The new information system which will be managing graphs, production reports, payroll records, etc., will now need an Information Technician.
Mr. Fly was hired to manage the IT department.
Mr. Ant, who once had been so productive and relaxed, detested this new plethora of paperwork and meetings which wasted most of his time. He became disenchanted, but he would not quit as he was hoping that it would get better over time.
His department's production target fell as a result, and then Mr. Lion decided that he needed a Department Manager for Mr. Ant's department.

The job was offered to Mr. Cicada, whose first decision was to buy carpet and an ergonomic chair for his office. Mr. Cicada also needed a computer and a personal assistant, whom he brought in from his previous department. She would help him prepare a Work and Budget Control Optimization Plan.
The widget department where Mr. Ant works now became a sad place, where nobody laughs anymore and everybody became stressed.

It was at this time that Mr. Cicada convinced Mr. Lion of the absolute necessity to start a climatic and motivational study of the environment.
Having reviewed the waning production reports, and the increased costs in running the production department, Mr. Lion decided to hire a consultant to study the operations.
Mr. Lion hired Mr. Owl who is a prestigious and renowned consultant to carry out an audit and suggest solutions.

Mr. Owl spent three months going over all the records of the department and came up with an enormous report in several volumes that concluded:

"THE DEPARTMENT IS OVERSTAFFED"

Mr. Lion now have a crucial decision to make, he will have to reduce staff.   He went down his list of employees and decided to fire the least productive.
Can you guess who gets canned first?
Remember the conscientious worker Mr. Ant who was the most productive individual in the company, and because of bureaucratic bungling became disenchanted and loss his motivation and productive capacity, he was the first to go.   His dismissal record was as follows:

"HE SHOWED LACK OF MOTIVATION, AND A
NEGATIVE ATTITUDE"

When you find a person, who knows their job and is willing to take responsibility, keep out of their way and don't bother the individual with unnecessary supervision.
When the work speaks for itself – don't interrupt.
What you may think is co-operation is nothing but interference.
– Thomas Dreier

As we keep adding new bureaucrats in needless positions without adequate professional ability, or hold them to specific performance, we dilute the efficiency of good governance. Too much cronyism allows people unfamiliar with the logistics of the operation to sabotage productivity, and no one can explain why we attract negative growth.
It's not a good time to be an ant.

Conceived and written by Ken Damally

ABC of Friendship

A Good Friend:

Accepts you as you are.
Believes in 'you'
Calls you just to say "Hello"
Does not give up on you
Envision the whole of you (even the unfinished parts).
Forgives your mistakes
Gives unconditionally
Helps you
Invites you
Just wants to "be" with you
Keeps you close at heart
Loves you for who you are
Makes a difference in your life
Never judges
Offers support
Picks you up
Quiets your fears
Raises your spirits
Says nice things about you
Tells you the truth when you need to hear it
Understands you
Values you
Walks beside you
Xplain things you don't understand
Yells when you won't listen, and
Zaps you back to reality - flexible people stays in shape.

A BRILLIANT ANECDOTE

It's more prudent to choose conference, cooperation, and humor, above conflict or confrontation.

Jason Danza was studying accounting at the Leeds College of Economics. HE WAS A MASTER OF REPARTEE, AND HIS QUICK WITTED AND SARCASTIC RESPONSES QUITE OFTEN GOT HIM IN SERIOUS TROUBLES.

A tenured professor name John Peters, disliked Jason intensely because he felt Jason was too smart for his pants, and so the Professor always displayed animosity towards him. Jason was such a confident young man, he would look Mr. Peters straight in the eye when addressing him, and never lowered his head. Although it was the polite thing to do, as Peters expected, there were always confrontations.

One day, Professor Peters was having lunch at the dining room when Jason came along with his tray and sat next to the professor.

The professor became indignant and said:
> *Mr Danza, don't you understand; [A pig and a bird do not sit together to eat]."*

Jason looked at him as a parent would on a rude child and calmly replied,
> *"You do not have to worry, professor. I'll fly away, and perch at another table".*

Mr. Peters, reddened with rage, decided to take revenge on Jason's next test paper, but Jason responded brilliantly to all questions.

The Professor was unhappy and frustrated, so he asked him some more questions:

> "Mr Danza, if you were walking down the street and found a package and inside was a bag of wisdom and another bag with a lot of money, which one would you take?"

Without hesitating, Jason responded;
> "The one with the money, of course."

The Professor smiling sarcastically said;
> "If I was in your place, I would have taken the wisdom."

Jason shrugged indifferently and responded,
> "Each one takes what he doesn't have."

Mr. Peters, by this time, was fit to be tied. So great was his anger that he wrote on Jason's exam paper the word "idiot" and gave it to Jason.
Jason took the exam paper and sat down at his desk, trying very hard to remain calm while he contemplated his next move.

A few minutes later, Jason got up, went to the professor and said to him in a dignified but sarcastically polite tone;
> "Mr. Peters, you autographed the sheet, but you did not give me a grade."

****

Jason got a job as a credit analyst at a prestigious accounting firm. One day he called a client about a delinquent account. The client was a bit perturb, and told Jason to shove the account up his rectum. Without skipping a beat, Jason responded;

"I will gladly do as you asked sir, but as soon as you remove your hand"

Life's Journey

Life is no straight and easy corridor along
which we travel free and unhampered,
But a maze of passages
through which we must seek our way,
lost and confused, now and again
checked in a blind alley,

But always, if we have faith,
a door will open for us,
not perhaps one that we ourselves
would ever have thought of,
but one that will ultimately
prove good for us.

By A.J. Cronin

Quiet Prayer for Everyone

THE PRAYER:

Father, Thank You for each and every day you have blessed us here on earth.   Thank you for your tender mercies.
Thank You for giving us friends and family to share joys and sorrows with.   I ask you to bless my friends, relatives, brothers and sisters in Christ and those I care deeply for, who are reading this anthology of poems this right now.
Where there is joy, give them continued joy.
Where there is pain or sorrow, give them your peace, happiness, and mercy.
Where there is self-doubt, release a renewed confidence in them so that they soar like an eagle.
Where there is need, fulfill their needs.
Bless their homes, families, finances, their goings and their comings.
Bless those who are holding a copy of this book that they will find it edifying and humorous.
Amen.

This page intentionally left blank

This page intentionally left blank

www.ingramcontent.com/pod-product-compliance
Lightning Source LLC
Chambersburg PA
CBHW070428010526
44118CB00014B/1948